BEST CAREERS FOR TEACHERS

Related Titles

Becoming a Teacher

PRAXIS I

TExES

BEST CAREERS FOR TEACHERS

Discover Alternative Options to Make the Most of Your Teaching Degree

LearningExpress®

NEW YORK

Published in the United States by LearningExpress, LLC, New York.

Library of Congress Cataloging-in-Publication Data:

Best careers for teachers : discover alternative options to make the most of your teaching degree.
    p. cm.
  Includes bibliographical references.
  ISBN-13: 978-1-57685-742-7
  ISBN-10: 1-57685-742-5
  1. Teaching—Vocational guidance—United States. 2. Education—Economic aspects—United States. 3. Life skills—study and teaching—United States. I. LearningExpress (Organization)
  LB1775.2.B44 2010
  370.23—dc22   2009045818

Printed in the United States of America

9 8 7 6 5 4 3 2 1

ISBN-13 978-1-57685-742-7

For more information or to place an order, contact LearningExpress at:
  2 Rector Street
  26th Floor
  New York, NY 10006

Or visit us at:
  www.learnatest.com

CONTENTS ||||||||||||||||||||||||||||||||||||||||||||||

BEST CAREERS FOR TEACHERS

INTRODUCTION

If you're looking through this book, you are either thinking about becoming teacher or you already are one (or someone you care about is!). Take a moment and read the next few paragraphs. Do any of the people described here sound familiar to you?

You have finally graduated, and in your hand is a brand new college degree with the ink not quite dry yet. All your years of hard work, from studying and taking tests to standing up in front of a classroom as part of your student teaching, are over. You are an official, certified *teacher* . . . but where do you go from here? Do you want a job working in the same school district you once attended as a student? Are you hoping to find a job on the other side of the country? Are you even sure you want to be in a traditional classroom setting or are you considering other, more out-of-the-box options? Maybe you have thought about teaching in a foreign country or virtual classes online. Decisions, decisions!

You have been teaching a couple of years now and, while you are enjoying it, it somehow feels like something is missing. You feel like you either need to change what you are doing or add something different to your usual schedule. Perhaps you're considering an entire change of pace—a new school, a different grade, another subject—or maybe you just want to supplement what you're doing with something different and exciting. It's time for a change!

You have been in the classroom for what sometimes feels like forever. It has been a rewarding career but you are ready to move on. You want to use the skills and knowledge you have accumulated over the years, but in alternative ways. You are positive that you could be excellent in another role, one that is related to teaching but not the same-old-same-old routine that you've maintained for a decade or more. What else is out there for someone like you?

Perhaps you love your teaching job and feel that it is one of the most rewarding professions on the planet, but you simply are not earning enough each month to make ends meet. You want to supplement your income—but it has to be in a way that doesn't interfere with or complicate your day job. How can you fit something else in that fits your talents and schedule and earns a decent paycheck?

Whether you are a graduate, a novice, a veteran teacher, or a satisfied teacher who needs a few extra bucks at the end of the week, you may find yourself looking for options outside the traditional classroom. This book can act as a guide to some possible career choices to mull over and maybe pursue.

"Approaching one-half of those who begin their training to become a teacher have left the profession before they have completed three years as a teacher."

—Margaret Adams, *How to Take Charge of Your Teaching Career*

Taking a Closer Look Inside

Let's start with a look at why you think you want to leave the classroom. There's nothing wrong with wanting to change the direction of your career. But before you make any big decisions, it is essential that you think through your reasoning and motivation and make sure your desire for a major career change is not just a momentary notion.

To get started, sit down, grab a piece of paper, and start jotting down answers to these questions. See what you learn about yourself in the process.

Why Do You Really Want to Leave the Classroom?

It is important that you can clearly articulate the reason—to yourself and to others. What specific details and/or examples would you include? How would you explain your decision to your parents, spouse/partner, best friends, or coworkers? How do you think they would respond? How would others' reactions affect your thoughts—if at all?

What Is Missing in the Teaching Experience for You Now?

Can you point to what it is you want but are not currently getting? If you can, is it a single factor or two that, if changed, would keep you in the classroom? Is this change within your power? If so, what can you do to change it. Is it worth the effort?

What Part of Your Teaching Job Brings You the Most Stress or Dissatisfaction?

Is it dealing with parents? Colleagues? The administration? Students? The paperwork? Is it the subject or grade level at which you are teaching? How could you change any of these factors?

Are You Sure You Want to Leave the Traditional Classroom?

What would happen if you could change schools, grades, or subjects? Would that be enough to make teaching in a classroom continue to be your first choice? If the answer is a possible "yes," then pinpoint which area has to change: Can you find another school district to teach in? Which one and why? Can you move up or down a grade? Can you switch subjects? What steps do you need to take in order to make any one of these things happen?

Has This Feeling about Changing Jobs Grown over Time or Is It in Response to a Recent Change?

If your dissatisfaction has been gradually increasing over months and years, it probably is valid. Make sure, however, that it is not a sudden response to a new curriculum, colleague, or administrative change. These factors often require an adjustment period and shouldn't spur you to a life-changing decision without adequate time to acclimate.

If Someone Told You Right Now That You Never Had to Step Inside a Classroom Again, What Would Be Your Initial Reaction?

If you immediately felt relief and a sense of freedom at this thought, it is a strong clue that you are truly ready for a career change. However, if your first response was regret and a profound sense of loss, you need to give this decision more thought and do more soul-searching.

Now that you have asked and answered these questions, you should have a clearer idea of where you stand professionally. Assuming you still want to pursue some type of career change, let's take time to evaluate all the skills and abilities your teaching career has taught you so far. The majority of these talents can be applied to a variety of other jobs—and they look great on the resume you will be constructing by the time you finish this book.

Who Am I?

Let's start with character traits. Some you were born with, some you acquired, and some you had to learn to survive as a teacher. Look at the list below. On a piece of paper, write down the traits that you know you have. On the other side of the paper, list the ones you may not have, but would like to work on developing. No one is looking, so don't worry about being modest. Instead, just be honest.

I Consider Myself to Be

optimistic	diplomatic
enthusiastic	trustworthy
communicative	observant
reliable	self-disciplined
punctual	energetic
personable	detail oriented
organized	attentive
committed	self-confident
motivational	a leader
compassionate	resourceful
empathetic	a negotiator
flexible	tenacious
perceptive	open-minded
knowledgeable	encouraging
creative	friendly
patient	a skillful time manager
humorous	determined
a team player	a good role model
healthy	intelligent

Want to know more about your abilities? Go online and put "aptitude tests" in the search box. You can find some insightful and fun tests. Check out the Career Assessment at www .careerexplorer .net/aptitude.asp or Career Tests at www.fun education.com.

How does your list look? Which side is longer? If you gave this list to someone who knows you well, how might it look different? What might they add or delete?

An Array of Skills

Next, ask yourself, what are your strongest skills? What are your areas of expertise? Naturally, the subjects you have taught within the classroom to students will come to mind first, but be sure to go beyond that. Think about workshops you have taught to others, fun classes you have shared with friends or your community, or even skills that you have shown your own children or your neighbors. How many areas do you actually specialize in? Every skill you have is one you can potentially teach to someone.

- **Communication:** Can you write a great essay? Letter? Research paper? E-mail? How about poems or short stories? Are you a master of punctuation, spelling, and grammar?

- **Speech:** Do you enjoy getting up in front of a crowd and talking? Are you clear and articulate? Can you keep an audience entertained and educate them, too?

- **Mathematics:** Does working with figures come easily to you? Do you know bookkeeping? Accounting?

- **Computers:** Are you a computer whiz who understands and enjoys learning about the latest developments in technology?

- **Science:** Do you have a solid working knowledge of basic scientific principles? Are you comfortable in a lab or even concocting things in a simple kitchen?

- **History:** Do you know what happened when, where it happened, and who was there? Can you make history relevant to modern students?

- **Sports and Fitness:** Can you play games well? Which ones? Do you know all the rules? Know how to teach them to others? Are you frequently at the gym or the track?

- **Arts and Crafts:** Do you know how to make things? Paint, draw, sculpt, and create? Are you able to help students find their inner creativity?

- **Foreign languages:** Can you read and speak another language? Can you sign?

- **Music and Dance:** What instruments can you play? Can you sing? Do you know various types of dance? Can you teach others these creative pursuits?

- **Cooking:** Are you a whiz in the kitchen? Can you bake or cook well?

- **Interior design:** Do you know what colors do and do not work together? Do you know the terminology of design and design history, like *art deco* and *early American style*?

- **Mechanics:** How are you at keeping the car in top condition and repairing appliances?

- **Construction:** Can you not only create a blueprint, but then also build what you designed?

- **Electronics:** Do you enjoy tinkering with both old and new forms of electronics? Do you know how things are put together? Can you take them apart?

- **Gardening/Landscaping:** What do you know about flowers and seeds? Planting fruits and vegetables? Can you design a backyard?

- **Photography:** What do you know about using a special telephoto lens or framing a photo when it is done? Do you know about different types of cameras? How familiar are you with both film and digital photography?

- **Environmental/Outdoor/Survival skills:** Can you pitch a tent in the pouring rain and prepare a three-course meal over the campfire? Do you know the skills needed to survive if you get lost in the process? What can you teach others about helping the environment? Are you familiar with the environmental problems facing the planet, and the steps we need to take to solve them?

- **Film and theatre:** Do you love drama on the silver screen and/or the stage? What do you know about lighting, props, and costuming? Are you familiar with the history of cinema and the theater? Are you really a closet director who can picture fantastic scenes before they happen?

- **Sales:** How adept would you be at selling a service or product? Do you have skills of persuasion and demonstration? Most teachers do, whether they know it or not.

Taking time to focus on your strengths and talents is the first step in pursuing additional work or a new career pathway. Keep them in mind as you read through the possibilities listed in the coming chapters. Also, have the list handy when it is time to come up with an updated resume.

Saying Good-Bye

If you decide that you are going to leave your current position, whether to go to a different school or on to a completely different career, be sure to leave on a positive note. Give your school administration at least 30 days notice so they have time to find a replacement. If appropriate, talk to your students as well. It is respectful to let them know what you're planning to do. How much you explain is up to you and how you connect with your classes, but don't just disappear.

Be sure to read your contract and follow whatever it says about quitting procedures and policies. If you aren't sure what they are or how to follow each one, talk to someone in human resources for clarification. You do not want to accidentally break a rule or cause a problem for anyone in the school (most importantly, the students).

Consider asking for reference letters from some of your coworkers and others in administration. They could come

"Poor earning potential, along with added stress caused by larger classrooms, and increased responsibility in and out of the classroom, have led to record numbers of teachers seeking work elsewhere."
—Margaret Gisler, *101 Career Alternatives for Teachers*

in quite handy when applying for another job. Also be sure not to burn your bridges behind you when you leave your school. Even if you happen to be leaving because you were unhappy with colleagues or the administration, do all you can to make it a friendly departure. You never know whether you might be returning in the future, plus networking is one of your biggest job search tools so contacts are important.

The decision to leave traditional classroom teaching is not an easy one, but it is the right one for many teachers. It is not a sign of failure of any kind; instead, it is a sign that your career is vitally important to you and is undergoing some adjustments. When learning something new—like finding another career, do just what you told your students—do your homework. Let's get started.

SECTION I

Options, Options Everywhere

Where can you take your talents, abilities, and experience? You have many choices—teaching involves multiple traits and skills that can be applied to different fields. Think about the skill sets you could develop and see how each one of the areas listed in the book could connect with them. Some are going to feel like a definite mismatch ("No way do I want to do that, thank you very much!"). Some are going to feel like a stretch ("I never thought of doing that, but it could be okay, I guess."). Some will hit a note of compatibility ("Sure, I can imagine doing that, at least for a while.") and hopefully, a few will ring true enough for you ("Yes! That sounds like what I have been looking for!") that you will pursue information beyond the scope of this book. Good luck!

(A note about these jobs: While a great many of these jobs can be achieved with just your teaching degree, some of them may demand additional education to fit certain state or job requirements. Please take time to note these and do additional research for your area. Also, while some of these jobs have clear-cut salaries or annual incomes that can be verified with sources such as the Occupational Outlook Handbook 2008–2009—www.bls.gov/OCO/—others do not and will vary greatly depending on your skills, your location, and other factors.)

CHAPTER ONE

PUBLISHING POSSIBILITIES

Regardless of what subject or grade level you have been teaching in school, writing has almost certainly played a large part in your job. Whether filling out student grade reports with your feedback, creating lesson plans, constructing a multiple choice test, commenting on a research paper, or e-mailing students directly on the computer, you were putting words together.

Did you enjoy the process? Are you known for writing well? Did you get a kick out of similes or smile when you added a bit of alliteration? If you taught any English classes, chances are the answer to all of these questions is yes. The students who actually grinned when assigned a research paper or were sincerely happy to be assigned a book report were often the same ones who went on to college and got a teaching degree in English. Sound familiar to you?

If working with words is fun for you and you have developed a strong sense of the basics (grammar, punctuation, spelling, etc.), you might look into a career in the vast world of publishing. There are many different directions to go, so let's explore some of the most common ones.

Editor

The job of an editor is to read, review, and revise another person's writing. It might be an advertisement, a feature article, a short story, or an entire book. In addition, editors review story ideas proposed to their publishing houses and decide whether or not to buy publishing rights. Often, they oversee the production process of the books they accept, taking them from idea to manuscript to bound book. Editors need to be able to provide feedback to writers that is helpful without being critical. It is their job to make a writer's work the best it can be through skillful guidance, suggestions, and revisions.

"When I ended up getting married straight out of college, I wasn't sure how I was going to use my teaching degree. I taught at community college for a while but then we had our first child and I wanted to stay home with her. I began freelance writing and loved it. By the time we had our fourth child, I was a full-time writer and author."
—Tami, Indiana

In the world of **periodicals** (magazines and newspapers) there are often a number of different editors on a team. For example, in a large city newspaper, you typically have an editor-in-chief or executive editor (who oversees all the other editors), assistant editors (who do whatever the executive editor asks), managing editors (who supervise all the writers), assignment editors (who hands out story ideas to writers), and copy editors (who check facts and correct errors). At small, community periodicals, it is not unusual for one person to wear all these editorial hats at once, doing everything from picking the stories and who will write them to double-checking for spelling errors and writing a last-minute headline.

One of the most common types of editors, naturally, is **book** editors, who can work on everything from traditional novels and nonfiction books to textbooks and academic books. The first requirement for this job is that you love to read. Simply enjoying a book is not enough, though; as en editor you will take this one step further and have to evaluate the quality of what you're reading and know how well it will fit in and sell within the market. The work doesn't end there, since most editors also spend time monitoring the book's progress, meeting with agents and authors, attending book fairs, preparing reports on sales, and controlling costs.

As a teacher, you will have an extra in if you choose to go into textbook editing, because you will be a built-in subject matter expert (SME). Your job will most likely include researching and proposing new products, working with authors and freelance writers, plus editing and revising workbooks, textbooks, instructor's guides, and CDs on a variety of educational topics. Some of the skills you will need to put to use include time management, self-direction, and interpersonal skills.

Unfortunately, the growth rate for editors is rather low, projected at only 2 percent between now and 2016. Wages for editors vary widely (editorial assistants may start around $28,000–$35,000 but editors who climb the ranks to the level of publisher or vice president can earn well over $100,000) depending on how much work they do, the size of one editor's list, or the monetary value of the cumulative list of books the editor is responsible for, and so on. The median rate per hour is just over $24 with an annual wage of $49,990.

As with any other job, there are drawbacks and challenges to being an editor. You will most likely take a pay cut in the beginning from what you were earning as a teacher. You will find that reading becomes more of a chore than a pleasure since it's now a job requirement and promotions are often long in coming.

Writer/Author

Have you dreamed of seeing your name on the cover and spine of a book? Have you imagined your byline in a major magazine's table of contents? You aren't alone—wow, are you not alone! Becoming an author is an exciting and worthwhile goal but you will be facing quite a bit of competition. It seems like everyone has a story they want to tell. However, if you can combine an ability to write well and reliably with expertise in certain matters, or you can research thoroughly and efficiently and know how to find the information you need, writing may be a great avenue for you.

Although most people associate writers with books, they often write for other venues such as magazines, websites, blogs, company newsletters, advertisements, radio and television scripts, and much more. Some writers are assigned topics to write by editors, while others come up with ideas and propose them. Many writers do both. Usually they spend as much time doing research and conducting interviews as they do writing.

The occupation of a writer is expected to grow at 10 percent between now and 2016, which is considered about average. The median salary is $53,070. About one-third of writers are not paid a regular salary, however. They are considered freelance and are self-employed. Authors of books are typically paid in a variety of ways: Some are paid a *flat fee* to write a book and then they are done. Others are paid *royalties*, or a percentage of each book sold. Still others are paid an *advance* (a large lump sum given before any work has started) to write and royalties as copies are sold. Writers can be paid by the hour, by the word, or by the project. Those details are worked out between the writer and the editor at the time of either acceptance or assignment.

Freelance writing has definite advantages and disadvantages to consider. On the plus side: You can do most of the work in your pajamas and work whatever hours you prefer; you learn a lot about the world on a daily basis; you have a wide variety of bosses to work with; your job changes often enough that boredom is rare to get bored; and you can schedule vacations and days off, for the most part, whenever you need them to occur. This may sound like heaven to you—or, after the structure of the classroom it may sound like a nightmare. You may not like a job with this much freedom built in. It depends on your personality and personal style.

On the minus, there are some definite ones. For example, with many writing jobs, there is no regular payday. Payment comes in the mail after you have finished each project and often does not come as quickly as you think it will. This can be exasperating and stressful, especially if you need that check for your rent or grocery money. Equally as frustrating can be the fact that you don't have any guarantee that when one job is finished, another one will come along. You might also want to pay quarterly estimated tax payments to avoid one hefty payment each April 15.

Journalist/Columnist

If you'd like to be part of writing for a newspaper, there are many different roles to pursue. Reporters investigate leads and tips, conduct interviews, do research, and create stories. If you are connected with many people and organizations throughout your community, this might be a great position for you. Reporters cover everything from accidents to elections, exposes to obituaries. If they are asked to write on a regular basis and include their own opinions and experiences on a continuing topic, they are usually referred to as a **columnist**.

Unfortunately, this field is not expected to see much, if any, growth between now and 2016, because print newspapers are scaling back in the Internet age. The median annual salary for this position is $33,470.

As with the other jobs, being a reporter has pluses and minuses. It is not always exciting—you rarely get to be the features writer or columnist in the beginning and instead may be stuck with more mundane chores like writing obituaries, covering the local dog shows, or updating the horoscopes. It can take months to years to move up through the ranks. Once you do, being a "star" reporter typically means being on call 24/7, having to drop everything to follow a story, do an interview, or get copy turned in on time.

Proofreader

If you are the type of person who spots spelling mistakes or punctuation errors on store signs or restaurant menus, consider being a proofreader. It is a proofreader's job to read printed manuscripts and other written copy to spot all errors in grammar, spelling, and style. It takes an eye for detail to succeed at this job and most proofreaders are expected to move quickly and efficiently, typically under tight deadlines.

Statistics show that this job will grow more slowly than average between now and 2016 and that the average annual wage is $18,000.

Technical Writer

Technical writers have to worry less about creating a clear metaphor than a clear diagram. They often are employed to write scientific reports full of numbers and formulas, or manuals full of specifications and detailed descriptions. They commonly write policies and procedures for companies, as well as instruction manuals on new products. Technical writers are assigned the job of taking complicated concepts and language and translating it so that the average reader can understand it. Many technical writers have strong backgrounds in science and math, so if you taught those subjects, this field might be ideal for you. Technical writers can be hired by business and trade magazines, industrial companies, and even the federal government, among other organizations.

Technical writing jobs are expected to grow about 20 percent between now and 2016. That is about double the average rate. The position is typically paid by the hour and the median rate is almost $30 per hour, with an annual wage of $61,620.

Other possibilities in the publishing world that you might want to explore include scriptwriter, indexer, literary agent, resume writer, and news correspondent. Regardless of which direction you go, you will need to know how to use a computer and software such as Microsoft Word, as well as simple machines like a fax machine, scanner, and printer. Writing involves a great deal of e-mailing, downloading, and transmitting of material. Most likely those skills are ones you learned years ago when creating unit studies, constructing lesson plans, and putting together exams.

Home Sweet Home Office

Depending on what job you pursue in the writing/publishing world, you may find that you will need to set up a home office. Working from home can be great—your place, your rules, your clothes, your kitchen close by. There is no commute to worry about and think of the gas money you could save!

Setting up a home office is not a cut-and-dried formula. It will depend completely on what you're doing, what equipment you need and what you already have, how much work you have, how many hours you will be working at home, how much room you can take over for the office, what family you need to work around, and so on. Here are some ideas to get started:

- Make a list of what equipment and supplies you will need for your job (computer, printer, scanner, fax machine, desk, chair, filing cabinets and files, etc.) and divide it up between what you already own and what you will need to purchase. Find out how much each item costs and then create a budget to purchase things as you need them.

- Figure out how much room you have in your place to fit an office. You might have to do some rearranging. Consider using unusual places like part of your laundry room or a corner of the kitchen. It should be someplace where you can ideally get away from everything else and concentrate. It should also have adequate lighting for you.

- Consider getting a separate phone line for your home business. This way no one else can be using it when you need it and when it rings, you know to answer professionally. You can also record a more official answering machine message that doesn't confuse customers/clients.

- If you have a home office, you will need to do some homework on how to keep track of your expenses and income for when tax time comes around. You can take a number of deductions that you may not be aware of—and you will need them because self-employment taxes can be tough.

Interested in this field? Ask yourself these questions and think about how the answers might affect your career decisions.

1. How much do you enjoy the process of writing?
2. Do you think you could write on a daily basis and still enjoy it?
3. Are you willing to write about topics you know nothing/little about?
4. How up-to-date are your word processing skills?
5. How good are you at information research?
6. Do you know how to conduct a quality interview?
7. Can you stick to tight deadlines?
8. Can you read a piece of writing and come up with helpful comments to improve it?
9. If you could write about anything you wanted to, what would you chose?
10. Where could you market that type of writing?

Putting your teaching talents to work in the writing world can be a great choice. It may take time to make a decent income, but it's a great way to use your creativity.

Further Resources to Investigate

Organizations
American Society of Journalists and Authors
1501 Broadway, Suite 302
New York, NY 10036
www.asja.org

Association of American Publishers
71 Fifth Avenue Second Floor
New York, NY 10003-3004
www.publishers.org

Small Publishers Association of North America
1618 W. Colorado Avenue
Colorado Springs, CO 80904
www.spannet.org

Association for Education, Communication and Technology
1800 N. Stonelake Drive, Suite 2
Bloomington, IN 47404
www.aect.org

Editorial Freelance Association
71 West 23rd Street, Fourth Floor
New York, NY 10010
www.the-efa.org

Society for Technical Communications
901 North Stuart Street, Suite 904
Arlington, VA 22203
www.stc.org

Websites

The Freelance Writing Jobs Network
http://www.freelancewritinggigs.com/

Journalism Jobs
http://www.journalismjobs.com/

Additional Reading

Baverstock, Alison, et al. *How to Get a Job in Publishing: A Really Practical Guide to Careers in Books and Magazines* (A and C Black Publishers, 2008).

Quick Easy Guides. *How to Find a Job in the Publishing Industry* (Quick Easy Guides, 2008).

CHAPTER TWO

ASSISTING HOME EDUCATORS

As a teacher, you have probably been aware of the move toward homeschooling or home education for some time. Although statistics are hard to pin down, estimates generally indicate that home education is growing at an average of 15 percent each year. According to the National Center for Education Statistics, in 2007 there were more than 1.5 million homeschooled students in the United States. And that number is almost certainly too low, as many homeschoolers do not register with the state and go unnoticed and uncounted.

Where You Can Fit In

As a teacher, there are a number of ways you can help the homeschooling families in your community through freelance work. Some of the services you can offer include:

- **Facilitating and administering required state tests in the family's home.** Homeschooling rules vary from state to state, so you can start by checking what the laws are in your state. For example, in a number of states, registered homeschoolers are required to have their children tested at set grade levels to make sure they are scoring in the same percentiles as their public school peers. As a certified teacher, you can administer these tests and help keep homeschooling parents on track with their requirements.

- **Tutoring.** Some homeschooling parents utilize tutors for certain subjects and may be looking for someone exactly like you. If you have the time and ability to travel around your region, consider the example of a former science teacher named Mr. Mack of Rock-It Science (http://www.rockitscience.com/). He bought an old school bus and remodeled it into a rolling science lab. He parks his lab and offers science classes of all types to homeschoolers and other children's groups. You can advertise your services in local homeschooling newsletters, curriculum stores, and bookstores. If there are any homeschooling conferences held in your area (check out http://homeschooling.gomilpitas.com/calendar/events.htm for current lists of nationwide conferences), you can talk to the coordinators to see if you can place a business card or flyer in their packets, or even appear as a vendor during the event. You can also go online and post on homeschooling message boards (ask the moderator for permission first). Ann Zeise, head of one of the most thorough and popular homeschooling websites on the Internet, offers a Yahoo! group for teachers/tutors/mentors and homeschoolers who want to get connected. (You can find it at http://homeschooling.gomilpitas.com/extras/A2Zmentors.htm.)

- **Coordinating field trips.** If you know a lot of fascinating places to tour and visit in your immediate area, you could act as a field trip coordinator for homeschoolers. You could take care of all of the details—for example, making reservations,

"The students I work with are some of the most polite and respectful I've ever seen," said Angie Heinze, a certified public school teacher who teaches science to homeschoolers at a church and at her home. "They thank me for every class. They help me clean up. They're a breath of fresh air."

—A to Z Home's Cool, "For Teachers Who Want to Tutor"

arranging transportation, paying for group tickets—and homeschooling parents would pay you for your time and effort.

- **Assisting in lesson plan construction and unit studies.** If you've had a lot of practice creating lesson plans and unit studies, you might be able to put this experience to use by showing parents (especially those new to homeschooling) how to do the same thing. You can recommend curriculum, guide toward resources, help them network with area experts, and much more.

- **Teaching workshops.** The sky is the limit on this one. Consider offering your services to the homeschooling community by offering to lead workshops on subjects such as creating lesson plans, planning a unit study, finding quality curriculum, doing research, and so on. Also, if you have expertise and experience working with kids with special needs (learning differences, autism, etc.), you may be able to help guide parents to specific resources they may not know about. You might also create additional materials to go with your workshops and sell them.

- **Acting as a local mentor/resource.** How much you can charge for these services depends on a number of factors. Consider how much of your time is involved, your travel costs, the expense of any materials, and so on. You can go online and check out how much tutors in your area are charging. For teaching workshops and classes, you can usually charge a blanket fee, depending on session length, what materials you provide, and your overhead costs. Do some research online and in your newspaper's classified and display ads to see what others are charging for comparable workshops. Keep in mind that many homeschoolers are operating on single incomes, so they will not be able to pay premium costs. You might even consider offering an introductory class for free just to entice others to sign up for more.

A Cautionary Note

Before you pursue this avenue, take a moment to analyze your feelings about homeschooling. Do you accept it as a valid educational choice, or something that only nutty, negligent parents do? If it is the latter, skip this whole career path. Homeschooling parents will pick up on your attitudes (even if you keep them unspoken), and word of this will spread far faster than word of your helpful services. If you are confused or annoyed by homeschoolers' motivations, take the time to talk with them. Politely ask questions and listen to their answers. Do your homework and read books about homeschooling. Pick up several copies of Home Education Magazine and read them from cover to cover. You will get a much better idea of what the homeschooling community and way of thinking is like.

Ziese, in her article, "For Teachers Who Want to Tutor," has some excellent advice when she writes,

"Working with homeschoolers in a natural learning situation can be a fun and rewarding occupation. It takes someone who is willing to think outside the box and not try to duplicate public schooling. Get into it with an attitude of 'I'll probably learn as much from these homeschoolers as I hope to teach them.' Plan for contentment and success not stress and failure, and the possibilities are limitless. We are willing to experiment with all sorts of joyful and loving forms of education. Just be willing to prove to us that you are, too." (http://homeschooling.gomilpitas .com/articles/021800.htm)

Interested in this field? Ask yourself these questions and think about how the answers might affect this career choice.

1. What is your overall attitude about homeschooling?

2. Do you know any homeschoolers personally that you could talk to?

3. Do you have connections throughout the community for setting up field trips?

4. Are you comfortable working with kids who have not been educated traditionally?

5. Would it be hard for you to treat parents as educational equals?

6. Are you okay with kids who see you as an equal, rather than an authority?

7. Do you enjoy leading workshops?

8. Could you learn a topic along with a student?

9. Are you able to teach a subject without a set curriculum but with just what you have at hand?

10. Can you easily translate "educationalese" into language everyone understands?

Further Resources to Investigate

Organization

Home Education Magazine/Home Education Press
P.O. Box 1083
Tonasket, WA 98855-1083
www.homeedmag.com/hem.html

Websites

A to Z Home's Cool
http://homeschooling.gomilpitas.com/

Homeschool Support Network
http://www.homeeducator.com/HSN/

Additional Reading

Dobson, Linda. *What the Rest of Us can Learn from Homeschooling: How A+ Parents Can Give their Traditionally Schooled Kids the Academic Edge* (Three Rivers Press, 2003).

Orr, Tamra. *Homeschooling FAQ: The 101 Questions Every Homeschooling Parent Should Ask* (New York: LearningExpress, 2010).

CHAPTER THREE

TUTORING TIME

Perhaps you still thoroughly enjoy the process of teaching but you're tired of the public school setting or having to deal with so many different students with different learning styles and levels. In that case, you might enjoy tutoring. Since the process is one-on-one, you get the chance to get to know each one of your student's abilities, strengths, and weaknesses. You can design lessons and homework that fit those parameters, rather than trying to create a plan to suit 25 or more students at the same time. Typically, you can work the hours you want to and you can establish a relationship with the student's parents.

Tutors are frequently in demand. There are almost always students who are looking for extra help in one subject or another. Others might be looking for extra assistance in preparing for a national standardized test like the ACT, PSAT, or SAT—college admissions are increasingly competitive and parents are well aware that a high test score not only can give their child the edge to get in, but also to possibly earn scholarship money.

One of the biggest advantages to tutoring is that you can try it out while you are still working in the classroom. You can use it to simply supplement your income or find out if you like the work well enough to transition into it full-time. To further branch out, you can experiment with teaching a different grade level and/or a different subject than you teach during the day. It will help you to figure out what you enjoy outside your typical professional routine and precisely what you are capable of—and what you're not. Perhaps most importantly, it will also give you some vital feedback on what the demand for tutoring is in your area. You don't want to leave your full-time teaching job just to discover that your city is overrun with qualified tutors and bereft of students needing help.

Creating a Plan That Works for You

Before you consider tutoring, think about your answers to the following questions. They will help you narrow down your focus and create a solid plan.

What Subjects or Topics Are You Willing to Tutor?

Certainly you can start with the subjects you taught or are currently teaching in school (and this might be the easiest route, as you can 100% prove your experience and expertise), but are there others that you know well enough to tackle as well? Think outside the classroom to that list of other talents discussed in the introduction.

Do You Want to Tutor One Subject or Several? What about Test Prep Tutoring?

All this will depend on how comfortable you are with subjects and now well you can market your skills to a potential client base. Can you do a little brushing up on some topics in order to expand what you have to offer? There are multiple test prep books available that you could spend time studying to familiarize yourself with the format and philosophy of the different standardized exams. You might have the basic background in the levels of math/science/reading/vocabulary/writing covered on the exams, but it is just as important when tutoring for standardized tests to teach students exactly what they need to do in order to pass a rigorous, timed, stressful, and high-stakes test. When the SATs and ACTs roll around, many parents start to look frantically for a quality tutor who can help their child get a high score or improve on a previous disappointing score.

What Age Group Do You Want to Tutor?

Again, you can stick to the grade level you are used to teaching in the classroom, but you don't have to. Would you prefer to work with older or younger kids? This is your chance to give it a try. Don't stop at kids, however. College students may want a tutor as well, especially if they have to brush up on topics they are required to study outside their major in order to graduate (like math or writing). Adult students returning to school can offer another opportunity.

Where Do You Want to Do the Tutoring?

Some people want to have students come to their own homes, while other tutors want to drive to the client's home instead, or meet in a public place like a library or a cafe. If you have students come to your house, you will need to have a quiet place to work, away from the rest of your family. If you go to their homes, you will have to factor in time for driving and money spent on gas. You will also have to think about how far you are willing to travel. In some tutoring situations, you might have a community center, church, library, school, or other learning center where you can teach your students.

How Much Should You Charge to Tutor?

This is not an easy question either, as there is no set amount. The rate you can and should charge varies depending on elements such as your years of experience, how many

"When your tutees realize that you tutor because you care and that you are genuinely interested in them and in having a strong tutor-tutee bond, tutoring becomes an experience filled with moments of pleasure, satisfaction, and joy.... Tutors often come out of their tutoring relationships with a much deeper sense of satisfaction than they had expected."
—Jerome Rabow, *Tutoring Matters*

hours per week you tutor, if you go to your clients or they come to you, how complex the subject matter is, and so on. Most tutors earn at least $20 an hour and if they have a teaching degree, they can commonly earn $30 to $40 an hour or more. In some areas, for the most experienced tutors, hourly rates can even top $60 or even $100 an hour! To set a beginning rate, get a sense of what your colleagues who teach at comparable levels charge. If you can, find out what tutors in your area tend to charge. You obviously don't want to go too much above that level to remain an enticing option. If you are just starting out, consider dropping a bit below this level. Once you prove you're legit and talented, you can raise your rates for new clients.

What Days and Hours Do You Want to Tutor?

How much time you want to spend tutoring is completely up to you, but it is important to remember that students only have certain times at which they will easily be able to meet with you. Typically, students will only be available after 3 P.M. on weekdays until 9 P.M. or so. Of course, weekends are open for both of you, but may be hard to find a chunk of time where you're both free and willing to work on your day off.

Getting the Word Out

Once you have worked out all the details listed above, you will need to focus on marketing your services. You can do this a variety of ways. When you first get started, you can advertise in a number of places including bulletin boards in churches, schools, grocery stores, teacher supply stores, and bookstores. You can also place a free ad on craigslist .com, as well as in local city and independent newspapers. In addition, consider having fliers, brochures, posters, and business cards created with your name and basic contact information on them. You can post these and hand them out in person. Talk to guidance counselors at the area schools and let them know what you have to offer.

Once you have some clients established, the best advertising you can possibly have is word of mouth. If your students and their parents are happy with your services, they will tell others and soon you will get more clients. You can also ask satisfied families to give you testimonials or reference letters that you can show others or use excerpts of in your advertising.

What You Need to Start

Your start-up costs for tutoring are quite minimal, which is another reason that it is an easy career to transition into. You will need simple files for keeping records on individual clients. You will most likely want to take notes on what each student and his or her parents want to achieve through the tutoring. You may also want to note each student's strengths and weaknesses. If you have permission to contact his or her teachers, you might want to find out what teaching methods have or have not been successful in the past. You will also want to have invoicing forms and handouts that clearly explain your payment structures and your personal rules and policies. A simple invoice is all that is necessary, and generic forms can often be found online or built into Microsoft Word.

The Drawbacks

There is no such thing as the perfect job and that is certainly true of tutoring—it is usually not a very consistent business. Work will most likely go up prior to the administration of big national tests like the SAT or ACT

"You have reached the stage in your life when you want to be your own boss and make choices about the way in which you work. Choosing to start your own tutoring agency will radically alter and enhance your lifestyle because you can make it fit around family or other work commitments, leisure pursuits and holidays."

—Gillian Stellman,
How to Start and Run a Home Tutoring Business

and drop when they are over. Scheduling can be a real pain; students have a tendency to forget, cancel, or postpone their sessions. You will have to be quite flexible (and most likely very patient) to succeed in this business. Tutoring is also quite different than teaching 30 students at the same time. It is important that you can adjust to individual learning styles and paces.

Tutoring is one of the best ways to keep connected with everything you have learned about teaching. It has low overhead and is almost always in demand. Give this new (or additional) career option some thought and see if it might be the right fit for you.

Interested in this field? Ask yourself these questions and think about how the answers might affect this career choice.

1. How do you handle one-on-one interaction as opposed to a classroom?

2. How up-to-date are you on the requirements of today's ACT and SAT exams?

3. How do you feel about working with adults instead of children?

4. What nonacademic subjects are you capable of teaching?

5. Are you comfortable having students in your home?

6. Do you have a reliable vehicle in case you go to another site to tutor?

7. Are you familiar with and able to adapt to different learning styles and paces?

8. Do you have connections that you could use for networking your services?

9. What places do you know of that would put up one of your fliers or brochures?

10. What is your opinion of tutors and the services they provide?

Further Resources to Investigate

Organization
National Tutoring Association
P.O. Box 6840
Lakeland, FL 33807-6840
www.natatutor.org

Websites
Tutoring jobs
www.jobs4tutors.com/
http://www.tutor.com/our-company/careers

Kaplan Test Prep and Admissions
http://www.kaptest.com/Teach_for_Kaplan/Overview/CS_teach_
about.html

Additional Reading
Lewis, Beth. *How to Start a Home-Based Tutoring Business: Home-Based Business Series* (Globe Pequot, 2010).

Stellman, Gillian, and Vivienne Howse. *How to Start and Run a Home Tutoring Business: A Complete Manual for Setting Up and Running Your Own Tutoring Agency* (How to Books, 2009).

CHAPTER FOUR

PROVIDING DAY CARE AND BEFORE AND AFTER SCHOOL CARE

Perhaps you truly love working with children, but not necessarily in the classroom. If so, providing day care for preschoolers or before and after school care for older kids might be a perfect job option for you. As more and more parents have become two-income families, the need for quality child care has grown. As a person with full teaching credentials, you could easily be considered excellent for the job. Whether you would need additional training or certification depends on where you work and how many children you will care for.

Day care workers shoulder a great deal of responsibility. After all, when a parent turns his son or daughter over to you, it implies a huge amount of trust. It will be your job, for several hours a day, to meet that child's basic needs, from physical and emotional to intellectual and social. Clearly the needs of infants are different than those of older children. For the youngest set, your job would primarily include feeding, changing, holding, and playing. Older children typically require organized activities of some kind to keep busy.

Exploring Your Options

What questions should you consider before going into any kind of day care? Let's explore a few.

"Child care providers, sometimes called day care providers, were originally considered responsible only for the children's basic care. Preschool teachers were responsible only for the children's educational activities. The separation in these major fields continues to diminish because of the growing knowledge that anyone who spends any amount of time with children does affect their learning, and they must also care about the children's basic needs."

—Renee Wittenberg, *Opportunities in Child Care*

What Age Children Are You Most Comfortable With?

Do you prefer to spend your day with babies? Children under the age of two? Preschoolers? Are you familiar with their needs? If you have spent most of your time teaching teenagers, for example, starting to take care of infants may seem like a welcome change, but if you don't have much experience, it can quickly turn to disaster. Infants demand a great deal of watching, and since they cannot communicate with you yet, they usually cry until you figure out the problem. On the other hand, older kids often require homework assistance and help developing social skills. They will also need to be fed snacks on a regular basis (most likely provided by the parents, but this is one of the many details you will work out upon reaching an agreement).

Where Do You Want to Provide Day Care/Before and After School Care?

Child care typically takes place in one of three locations. Many people choose to open up their own homes. They designate certain parts of their homes for the business (creating a nice tax deduction in the process), and watch as many children as their state allows (laws vary on how many children per adults are allowed and are traditionally based on the age of the children). This type of child care is known as family child care. Some states require that your home be licensed if you are going to watch children as a business. They may conduct a background check on you, plus require that you are certified in CPR and first aid. If you choose this type of care, you will need to make sure you have the right supplies on hand. While infants do not have many needs (bottles, formulas, and diapers should be provided by the parents), older children will need a steady supply of games, arts, and crafts to hold their attention—and keep them out of trouble.

Another type of child care, private household care, is done in a client's home. This type of caretaker is sometimes known as a nanny or au pair, or simply a babysitter. In this situation, you will work one-on-one with a child or with siblings. Some child care workers work only during the daytime hours, while others live at the client's home and commonly must work on weeknights and weekends. If you are single, this can be a good arrangement. Nannies typically make $10 to $16 an hour, depending on their experience and the age and number of children involved.

The third type of child care is done in a kind of center, like a community center, church, public school, or large office building. In this situation, you would be more likely to share the care of children with several other people. Often you will need additional training or certification to get this job, so check state requirements. You will also have to deal with unannounced visits from the state licensing board, during which they will go through processes like measuring the square footage, asking the children about their activities, watching to make sure children are never left unobserved, inspecting the playground, and observing all caregiver interactions with the children. Health inspectors also come by without warning to test water temperatures, check supplies, and to make sure that all dangerous medicines and cleaning supplies are locked up safely.

Are You More Interested in Being a Child Care Provider or a Child Care Director?

The positions are similar. If you run your own child care business alone, you will have to take on some of director duties anyway. In a center, however, a director has quite a bit of responsibility, and is often given the tasks of supervising all providers, plus many administrative duties like:

- promoting enrollment
- ordering materials, equipment, and supplies
- conducting staff meetings
- hiring and firing providers and any other staff
- filling in if or when necessary
- receiving and recording tuition
- marketing and advertising
- establishing policies and procedures
- following all state regulations
- keeping the center clean and maintaining supplies and equipment
- maintaining contact with parents through meetings, notes, and/or conferences
- updating files on each child to record progress or problems

Are You Willing to Get Additional Training?

Many places will not require more than a teaching degree, but each state has its own requirements, which may include a national Child Development Associate credential or the Certified Childcare Professional designation from the Council for Professional Recognition and the National Child Care Association.

How Do You Feel about Working a Real Split Shift?

If you decide to work in before and after school child care, your work hours may be quite strange. Before school care means being at work as early as 6 A.M. and being finished by 10 A.M. A good portion of your day is then free, until you have to return for the after school care from approximately 2 P.M. to 6 P.M. You may love this schedule—you have hours each day to get things done—or you may despise it.

Finally, Are You Easily Grossed Out?

While it's true that as a teacher you might have already had opportunities to deal with bodily fluids of all kinds, in day care, you are sure to deal with such pleasures! If coping with urine, feces, blood, or vomit bothers you to the point that you might refuse to deal with them, this isn't the direction to go unless you have older kids in your charge—and then there is still no guarantee.

"Those privileged to touch the lives of children and youth should constantly be aware that their impact on a single child may affect a multitude of others a thousand years from now."

—Anonymous

The Drawbacks

Child care is rewarding work—like teaching, you get the chance to nurture and guide young people. But it has definite drawbacks, too. It is frequently a very high-stress job. Children can be physically and emotionally exhausting. Dealing with parents can also be challenging. The skills you have learned during your years in the classroom will help you here. You might have already dealt with fighting kids, angry parents, long hours, and maybe even very serious issues like possible abuse, so you most likely have an arsenal of coping techniques and helpful responses at your disposal.

The outlook for child care is quite high, with an average of 18 percent growth between now and 2016. The median annual income in 2006 was $17,630, although child care workers who work in residence and centers tend to make about $3,000 more per year.

Interested in this field? Consider the following questions and think about how your answers might affect this career choice:

1. What age children do you enjoy working with most?

2. Do you prefer to work one-on-one or with a group of children?

3. Would you prefer to be the only child care provider, or work with several others?

4. How much experience have you had with different aged children?

5. Would you prefer to focus on watching the kids or having more control over the center, as with a director's position?

6. Are you willing to work on weekends and holidays?

7. Can you take children on regional field trips? Would you want to?

8. Are you familiar with special needs children and what they require?

9. Does your state require that your home be licensed in order to operate a day care? If so, can you meet all of the requirements?

10. Is your family willing to work around your child care business?

Further Resources to Investigate

Organizations
National Association of Child Care Professionals
P.O. Box 90723
Austin, TX 78709
www.naccp.org

National Child Care Association
1325 G Street NW, Suite 500
Washington, DC 20005
www.nccanet.org

National Child Care Information Center
243 Church Street NW, Second Floor
Vienna, VA 22180
www.nccic.org

International Nanny Association
191 Clarksville Road
Princeton Junction, NJ 08550-3111
www.nanny.org

Council for Professional Recognition
2460 16th Street NW
Washington, D.C. 20009-3575
www.cdacouncil.org

Websites
The Original Nanny Jobs
www.nannyjobs.com

Great Au Pairs
www.greataupair.com/

Nanny Classifieds
www.nannyclassifieds.com

Additional Reading

Eberts, Marjorie and Margaret Gisler. *Careers in Child Care* (New York: McGraw-Hill, 2007).

Wittenberg, Renee. *Opportunities in Child Care Careers* (New York: McGraw-Hill, 2006).

CHAPTER FIVE

COUNSELING AT CAMP

Just when you thought you would never have to sing another silly song or pull out yet another arts and crafts activity, you might begin thinking about working as a camp counselor. Perhaps you have warm and wonderful memories of going to camp as a child, or you have seen your students or your own children go to camp and come home full of great stories. Maybe you always wanted to go to camp when you were little and didn't get the opportunity. Now you might have the chance. Consider becoming a counselor at one of the day or resident camps in your area, or even an extended (two to six weeks) camp offered in various places throughout the world.

Keep in mind as you consider this option that being a camper is nothing like being a camp counselor. Sure, it is still fun and you get to participate in a variety of enjoyable outdoor activities, but it is not a week or two—or an entire summer—full of fun and games. It is hard work and a huge amount of responsibility. Also keep in mind that many of these positions are held by college students or young-20s—usually former campers themselves. A number of camps would be thrilled, however, to have someone as skillful as a former teacher working at their camps. Apply and show them what you have to offer!

The Nitty Gritty of Being a Camp Counselor

Let's look at some questions you need to think over before you consider packing your sleeping bag and bandanas.

What Background Skills Do You Bring to This Job?

Clearly you know how you can incorporate your academic skills into camp activities in order to teach kids, but what else can you bring to being a camp counselor? Are you certified in CPR and First Aid? If not, it would be a good idea to take some classes. Do you have any lifeguard training? It would be helpful. Have you played a variety of sports in the past? You may be called on to teach the basics to many kids very soon.

Are You Physically Fit? Are You Willing to Get Fit?

This job is one in which you will spend virtually no time relaxing. Sure, there are mealtimes and even rest periods, but chances are they will be filled with you running around to get all those things that were lost or forgotten or suddenly desperately needed. You need to have the physical stamina for a job where you chase kids. Unless you are a camp counselor at a computer, science, or academic camp, you will most likely get a better workout being a camp counselor than any gym membership can buy.

How Do You Feel about Mother Nature?

If you are creeped out by spider webs, drop to the ground if hear a bat, and constantly worry that that odd sound you keep hearing really is a hungry coyote circling the camp,

"Education and camping are great fields of endeavor. There is much opportunity for creativity and for positively affecting the future lives of our children and hence our planet. It is extremely rare to find a field where so much good can be accomplished for oneself and for others."

—Mark Richman, *The Ultimate Camp Counselor Manual*

then being a counselor is probably not the best option for you. You have to enjoy all of Mother Nature, from the unexpected thunderstorms to the hairy moths that follow your flashlight wherever it goes. You are a role model for a lot of young people, so if you look scared, they may be terrified.

What Outdoor Skills Have You Developed?

How much personal camping experience have you had? Do you know how to pitch a tent? How about if it is pouring down rain? Can you start a fire? Cook over the fire? Put out the fire? Can you read and follow a compass? Chances are you would be working in a camp where kitchen facilities provide most of the food, but you have to know how to make s'mores over an open campfire, just in case. You will have access to showers and bathrooms in most cases, but if you don't, do you know how to find the water you need?

How Much Do You Know about These Activities? How Much Would You Have to Learn?

Take a look at this list and ask yourself whether you are a novice, a veteran, or would rather pay someone else to do it in your place.

- canoeing
- kayaking
- swimming
- hiking
- horseback riding
- arts and crafts
- archery
- camp songs

- music
- drama
- storytelling

If you are planning to work at a specific type of camp, clearly you will need to be somewhat of an authority on a specific topic. There are computer camps, science camps, math camps, and of course, sports camps. Thousands of kids spend their summers learning how to be better tennis/soccer/basketball players, and if you happen to know a sport well, this can be a great opportunity to help.

A good camp counselor can be hard to find, so you may find camp directors thrilled to discover your interest in the job. Your experience working with children will be of great importance. Camp directors are searching for people who can nurture kids while remaining somewhat distant. Creating rapport without becoming a "friend" is a skill that you have already developed from your years in the classroom.

Other skills that you have learned as a teacher will serve you well at camp. You need to know your campers' names as fast as possible to establish a connection. (Seating charts don't work at camp.) You have to memorize the camp's daily schedule so you always know where you and your campers are supposed to be at any point in time. Planning and organizing a variety of activities will be a regular duty. While your director (and hey, you can always aim for that job instead!) often does the majority of it, you will certainly be called on spontaneously to fill in an unexpected time gap with a game, song, or craft. Having a repertoire of on-the-spot activities at your mental fingertips is a great skill to develop.

Other abilities found in great camp counselors and directors include an ability to motivate others, a consistent awareness and sensitivity to campers' feelings and moods (watch for homesickness—it's a regular!), and teaching such subjects (through lessons and role modeling) as getting along with others, developing strong relationships, accepting differences in others, sharing and cooperating, creating self-sufficiency, and making group decisions. All of these sound mighty familiar, of course, because they are the same skills you have been implementing in your classroom for years.

"The ability to be sensitive to the needs of all the campers is a very important aspect of a good camp counselor. Camp counselors must be able to read verbal and nonverbal signals from within their groups. All directors want their staff to recognize when a child is not connected to their peers or is melancholic. . . . The need to read individuals and understand their thoughts and feelings takes great patience and attention. Counselors must be willing to listen to their campers in order to understand how they are feeling. Empathy, along with the understanding of how others are feeling, is a skill that is priceless in our society and is highly desirable for camp directors."
—Greg Schreiner, director of Buckley Day Camp

The Endless Options Available

Where can you find camping jobs? It depends on where you want to go. If you want to stay reasonably near where you live, you can check out:

- Boy Scouts
- Girl Scouts
- Camp Fire USA
- Boys and Girls Club
- churches
- preschools and elementary schools
- community organizations (YWCA/YMCA, etc.)

If you are willing to travel, you can connect with some of the national and international camp organizations. (See the list at the end of this chapter.) These opportunities are usually more involved, last longer, and while they may not pay more, they do afford you the chance to travel.

If you are still not sure if camp counselor is a good fit for you, keep in mind how many different types of camps there are. Here is a limited list.

Sports Camps

While some of these are generic, most specialize in a particular sport such as tennis, soccer, golf, track, martial arts, or basketball. Obviously you need to know how to play the sport very well and be able to teach new skills, strategies, moves, and techniques. Want to know more? Check out http://www.ussportscamps .com/.

Religious Camps

Camps based on a variety of faiths are sponsored by many different churches and other religious organizations. You should personally follow whatever faith is represented at the camp and be willing to take part in daily devotionals and other religious practices. You can find listing of camps like these at http://www .mysummercamps.com/camps/Religious_Camps/Christian/ index.html.

Fitness Camps

Once not so delicately known as fat camps, these camps emphasize physical activity and nutritious food. As a role model, you should have a commitment to fitness, eating right, and maintaining a healthy lifestyle. You will be called on motivate campers through the very tough struggle of losing weight—it is essential to have a cheery attitude and the ability to relate to children with self-esteem issues. You can find information on these camps at http://www.mysummercamps.com/camps/Sports_Camps/Fitness/index.html.

Academic and Extracurricular Camps

Themed summer camps can concentrate on basically any special topic you can think of, like computers, drama, music, writing, and many more. It is important that whatever the theme is, you have a strong background in it and can present additional guidance and education. The sky is really the limit for the types of camps available all around the country—they include anything from video game design and digital photography to environmental studies or aviation. To find out more about these, put the theme you might be interested in counseling and the word "camp" in any search box. For example, for academic camps, you might check out http://www.allensguide.com/academic.

Special Needs Camps

These camps, designed for children with physical or mental disabilities, make sure that all children get the chance to enjoy the experience of summer camp. Typically, staff is specially trained in how to cope with the special needs of the campers. If you already have experience in this area, you will have a real leg up on getting a job. A recent news story covered a camp in the Catskill Mountains (Camp Our Voice) for kids who stutter but want to pursue a career on the stage or behind the podium. You can find a list of camps across the country at http://www.veryspecialcamps.com/.

Adult Camps

Of course, not all camps are for kids. There are a number of camps for adults who want to get away for a weekend or so, need rehabilitation from drug and/or alcohol abuse, want further instruction in a sport or other personal goal, and much, much more. Some adult camps offered are quite quirky and fun, too, including:

- Rock'n' Roll Fantasy Camp, a five-day fantasy camp offered in New York City, Las Vegas, and London

- Crush Camp, a three-day camp in California that teaches adults how to take wine from vine to glass

- Atlantic City's World Poker Tournament Boot Camp, a camp in which players learn better card playing techniques

- Gladiator Training, a three-hour camp in Rome on combat techniques—in costume!

- Elephant Mahout Training, a three-day camp in Northern Thailand to learn about elephant care

- Space Camp, a three- to eight-day camp in Huntsville, Alabama that simulates astronaut training and an actual shuttle mission

- Ghost Hunter University, a two-day camp in New Orleans that teaches campers all about the basics of ghost hunting

- Crossword Puzzle Creation Camp, a seven-day camp and cruise through the Caribbean featuring tricks on puzzle-solving skills and vocabulary development

- African Vet Safaris, a four- to five-day camp in South Africa that shows the ins and outs of wildlife veterinary work

Other examples of adult camps include the Crow Canyon Archaeological Center in Colorado, the Santa Fe Photographic Workshops in the Sangre de Cristo Mountains, and the Second City Training Center camps in Chicago, Illinois.

Boot Camps

Typically, these camps are designed for young people who have been in trouble with the police, their parents, school, and more. Working at these camps often requires special training in how to handle disobedient or angry campers, and you may also need special clearances. Look for information at http://www.bootcampsforteens.com/index.html and http://www.bootcamps.com.

Day Camps

While all the other camps listed here tend to be residential camps, most communities also offer a number of day camps as well. There are not usually as many job openings at these and they tend to pay less, but you also get to go home at the end of the day and take a shower. You can search for these locally or through the website http://www.daycamps.net.

A Camp for Children of Soldiers

A current innovation in camps is those held specifically for the children of deployed soldiers. Organized by the nonprofit National Military Family Association, based in Alexandria, Virginia, they are designed for any of the 230,000 American youth who have a mother or father fighting in the war. While many of the activities are the same as at any camp, there are differences. In one camp, kids make lists of the ways their lives differ from the lives of their peers whose families aren't part of the military. Campers get chances to discuss how hard it is to have a parent gone all the time—and in danger. Counselors at these camps require special training to help the campers who are under this constant stress.

Compensation

You can gain a great deal from being a camp counselor, but unfortunately, it will not be financial gain. Some

"In recent years, the number of specialized camp opportunities for adults has grown significantly. Camp isn't just for kids anymore. In a hectic world, it offers an oasis, with opportunities for learning in a fun environment. Many adults find a camp vacation to be more rewarding than a week at a resort."
—Peg L. Smith, chief executive officer of The American Camp Association

positions pay more than others, of course. The camp director or nursing staff, for example, will have slightly higher paychecks. According to the American Camping Association, for example, average salaries are:

- head counselor: $310 per week
- camp counselor: $230 per week
- camp nurse: $430 per week
- cook and staff: $300 per week

(Most of these positions also come with three meals a day and camp shelter—that is, "room and board.")

Summer camp directors, who put in hours all year round, typically make about $40,000 a year with benefits.

The outlook for this job is strong because summer camp enrollment increases about 10 percent each year. Do not think of the job as a summer-only position, however. Almost three-quarters of all camp directors work full time. Imagine a whole year of going to camp—pass the mosquito repellent!

Interested in this field? Consider these questions and think about how the answers might affect this career choice:

1. Do you prefer the idea of day camp or resident? What age children?

2. Do you like the idea of staying in your area or traveling to other parts of the world?

3. Can you cope with a job that tends to hire only on a seasonal basis?

4. Have you been trained in CPR and first aid? Have you had any lifeguard training?

5. How much experience have you had with outdoor skills?

6. Are you a high maintenance or a low maintenance person?

7. Do you remember names well?

8. How do you tend to respond in emergency situations? Does the sight of blood bother you at all?

9. How many camp songs do you know? Do you know how to track down a lot more?

10. Are you bug or germ phobic? (Hint: If so, this is probably not the right field for you.)

Further Resources to Investigate

Organizations
National Recreation and Park Association
22377 Belmont Ridge Road
Ashburn, VA 20148-4501
www.nrpa.org

American Camping Association
5000 State Road 67 North
Martinsville, IN 46151-7902
www.acacamps.org

National Camp Association, Inc.
610 5th Avenue
P.O. Box 5371
New York, NY 10185
www.summercamp.org

Websites

Camp Counselor and Summer Camp Staff Positions
http://www.campchannel.com/jobboard/

Great Camp Jobs
http://www.greatcampjobs.com/

Camp Counselors USA
www.ccusa.com

Camp Depot
http://www.campdepot.com/JS_DirectorsMeassages.html

Additional Reading

Richman, Mark. *The Ultimate Camp Counselor Manual: How to Survive and Succeed Magnificently at Summer Camp* (iUniverse, Inc., 2006).

Schnell, Jim. *The Camp Counselor's Guide to Interpersonal Communication* (Healthy Learning, 2009).

Wolk, Josh. *Cabin Pressure: One Man's Desperate Attempt to Recapture his Youth as a Camp Counselor* (Hyperion, 2007).

CHAPTER SIX

COACHING ATHLETES AND OTHERS

When you were working in the public school system, did you have a colleague who somehow got drafted into being the sports coach along with teaching regular classes? A large number of high school coaches are teachers who were asked to coach—or, actually, sometimes coaches who were asked to teach. The two professions definitely seem to go hand-in-hand.

Applying Your Teaching Skills to Coaching

It is understandable why the two jobs are often combined. After all, being a good coach utilizes many of the same qualities and skill sets as being a good teacher. Chances are if you are hired to be the school's coach, you may well also be the PE, or gym, teacher. Be sure to ask about that during your initial job interview so it doesn't come as a surprise down the line. Now, let's look at what questions you might want to think about before taking this career route.

What Is Your Personal Experience with Sports? Which Ones?

Have you played sports as long as you can remember? Have you been a member of either a school team or an outside organization? Are you familiar with team dynamics and the drama that can ensue when a group of athletic, competitive people are put together in a big group? Reading about sports and watching endless games on television or even in the stands is important, but personally knowing what it feels like to be in the game is far more relevant. The more you have experienced, the better coach you are likely to be.

How Much Do You Know about Motivating Others?

One of the biggest parts of being a good coach is knowing how to motivate each player to do his or her best, whether to hit the ball harder or further, or run just a little bit faster. These are the same skills you used in the classroom as you encouraged your students to try harder, study longer, or listen more closely.

How Do You Handle Disciplining Your Team or Players?

Perhaps you relate coaching with an image of the angry sideline "cheerleader," screaming after every play and reminding players of what they've done wrong in an often humiliating way. This may work well for some teams and coaches, but most probably not with many. Are you familiar with different ways of discipline and motivation that you could apply as a coach? Are you willing to research them?

Can You Spot a Potential Athlete? Do You Know What to Do with a Former Superstar Who Is Struggling?

One of the best skills a coach can develop is the ability to look at young people and spot the most likely to be

"Coaching is unlocking a person's potential to maximize their own performance. It is helping them to learn, rather than teaching them."

—John Whitmore, *Coaching for Performance*

the star basketball player or the fastest runner. This one has a great arm; that one has an amazing kick. Scouting for new players is an integral part of the job. At the same time, you have to be able to help the other players who may be struggling to improve their game. You will need to develop realistic goals for each person, as well as create drills and practices that will improve everyone's abilities. It is a lot like creating lesson plans, but with a higher emphasis on individuality.

How Do You Respond to Competition?

Do you enjoy competing? Almost more important (because it's much tougher), how do you feel about losing? It is important that you provide your athletes and/or team with a good role model in the face of losses. One of the most vital lessons that anyone should learn when playing any sport is the element of good sportsmanship.

What other responsibilities will you have as a coach? You will need to:

- teach the basics of multiple sports
- develop winning game strategies
- select, purchase, and store necessary sports equipment, materials, and supplies
- work irregular hours and be at games on weeknights and weekends
- be available to your athletes/team members when they need you
- teach elements of form, techniques, endurance, and skills
- join school sports associations
- represent the school during intramural competitions
- direct team strategies and call out your recommended plays during games

"Many coaches are afraid to pick who they want to coach. They worry that they are walking away from something, such as a missed opportunity or potential clients. They worry that they are being too narrow or limiting by specializing. What you really walk away from is an unproductive strategy. You cannot coach the whole world successfully."
—Deborah Brown-Volkman, *Four Steps to Building a Profitable Coaching Practice*

Compensation

The job outlook for coaches is just slightly above the national average for other jobs. The average yearly income for coaches is $26,950, although it is typically a bit higher if coupled with teaching other classes. Keep in mind that schools are only one place to coach. You might check into local fitness and recreation centers, community parks, and community organizations like the Y for potential jobs.

Being a coach is a wonderful way to blend guiding children and playing sports. However, there are some important drawbacks to consider. You will frequently put in amazingly long hours, especially during the season during which your sport is busy competing. It typically involves a fair amount of travel, which can mean time away from your family. It takes an ongoing dedication and passion that can be quite tiring, both physically and mentally.

Beyond the Field

Take time to do some brainstorming outside the box when it comes to coaching. Not all coaches teach athletics. There are a number of other types of coaches and each one involves the same basic talent: the ability to direct, instruct, and train an individual or team/group with the goal of developing and improving on a skill. For many people, coaching has become a very lucrative job, as the overhead and training is limited

What coaching jobs exist that don't involve keeping score? There are life coaches (What's missing in my life and how can I find it?); career coaches (Where do I go from here with these skills?); health coaches (Can I eat better and/or exercise more effectively?); date/relationship coaches (Where do I meet that special someone?); and childbirth coaches (When do I need to breathe and how fast?). Let's take a brief look at each one.

Life Coach

This field has seen tremendous growth in recent years. The International Coach Federation has more than 12,000 members worldwide, double what it had only five years earlier. The idea of life coaching got its start in the executive world (leadership and management training) and expanded from there. Virtually everyone has goals in life—things they want to accomplish but need extra or expert support and guidance to attain. That is where the life coach comes in. He or she is there to help you quit smoking or start exercising, improve your marriage or decrease your unnecessary stress. Currently, there is no required education or training program to complete for this job. It is not regulated by any agency. Some organizations offer a type of certification, but it is not necessary to have to hang out a life coach shingle with your name on it. To see a listing of current life coaches, check out http://www.lifecoach.com/.

Career Coach

Just like its name implies, a career coach is someone who helps others discover the best possible profession they are suited for and then get jobs in those markets. They ask questions, provide tips and resources, and help network in order to see their clients get just the right jobs. Typical responsibilities of this type of coach include assessing your

"If you are frustrated with an aspect of your life, not sure how to stop making the same choices you keep making, or just want to have more happiness, peace of mind, and passion—life coaching can do that for you."
—Rhonda Briitten, founder of the Fearless Living Institute

behavior, creating an action plan, eliminating distractions, providing guidance, and teaching helpful information on creating resumes, doing interviews, and marketing yourself. Look into this profession through http://www .careercoachinstitute.com/.

Health Coach

As the focus on becoming a healthier nation grows, so does this field. A health coach traditionally focuses on helping a person improve his diet and/or fitness, while others emphasize helping people with specific conditions or illnesses to live longer and better. This type of coach may give advice on vitamin supplementation, ways to reduce stress, or how to stop smoking. To find out more about the field, check out http://www.healthcoachtraining .com/.

Dating/Relationship Coach

Are you a great matchmaker? You might want to look into becoming a dating coach. This type of coach focuses on helping clients meet and attract compatible mates, whether for the short term or for a long-term relationship. The job may include lessons in everything from effective flirting to fashion faux pas. Typically, dating coaches do not arrange dates, but instead guide clients to making their own. You can see more about the profession at http:// www.datingcoach.net.

Childbirth Coach

Do you love being around moms and babies? This may be a great avenue to pursue. (Please note that many labor/childbirth coaches are also known as doulas.) This type of coach is trained to assist women before, during, and after

> "We have business coaches, dietitians, accountants, but we don't have an expert for our love life? It doesn't make sense. It is really the single most important aspect in our life."
>
> —Lisa Clampitt, founder of the Matchmaking Institute, New York

labor and delivery. Many doulas help with the non-medical aspects of prenatal care, answering questions, easing fears, and helping parents develop a birth plan. They often teach mothers-to-be how to breathe during the birthing process and may teach classes on various methods such as Lamaze or Bradley techniques. During labor itself, doulas typically assist with breathing through contractions. Some are trained in using homeopathy or other alternative health care with laboring women. Doulas may provide massage and, in home birth cases, help manage other children—and confused husbands. After the baby is born, some childbirth coaches stay in the hospital or home to help establish breast-feeding, instruct new parents on how to hold and care for their new child, and generally make sure the new family is secure. Doulas are not usually paid by the hour but in a lump sum that can run hundreds to thousands of dollars, depending on the area, the extent of the services, and the time involved. Training is not required but is often requested by clients; programs can be found online and through local childbirth organizations. Check out http://www.dona.org/mothers/index.php for more information.

Coaching—on and off the field—means a great deal of time and dedication on your part. Not only do you have to be skilled in whatever topic it might be, but you also have to have personal passion to help another person achieve his or her goals. Your hours will most likely not be very predictable and your paycheck might fluctuate greatly from week to week, depending on how many clients you have. You may find yourself being a combination of therapist and coach at the same time, and it can be draining and demanding. On the other hand, if you see someone blossom and achieve something new—from a personal best score to the perfect job—and know that you were a big part of that achievement, it's a feeling you will never forget. Getting paid for it just makes it that much better.

Interested in this field? Consider these questions and think about how the answers might affect this career choice:

1. What sports do you know extremely well? Are you familiar with the elements of teamwork?

2. What is your fitness level? Can you keep up in the classes you would teach?

3. Are you willing to coach individual teams after school and on weekends?

4. What sports have you personally played in your life? Have you been on a team?

5. What are your philosophies on competition?

6. Have you had any additional courses in sports psychology, physiology, kinesiology, nutrition and fitness, physical education, or sports medicine? If not, would you be willing to take some or all of these courses?

7. Do you want to be a sports coach or does some other type of coaching appeal to you? If so, what kind and where can you find additional information about it?

8. What are your theories or ideas on disciplining your team members?

9. What types of motivation techniques would you use with your athletes?

Further Resources to Investigate

Organizations
American Coaching Association
2141 Birch Drive
Lafayette Hills, PA 19444
www.americoach.org

International Coach Federation
2365 Harrodsburg Road, Suite A325
Lexington, KY 40504
www.coachfederation.org

The National High School Coaches Association
3276 Nazareth Road
Easton, PA 18045
www.nhsca.com

National Association of Sports Officials
2017 Lathrop Avenue
Racine, WI 53405
www.naso.org

Websites
Coaching Jobs
http://www.coachingjobs.com/

Coaching Jobs
http://www.icoachusa.com/coach-membership-benefits/

Coaching Jobs
http://www.schoolspring.com/find/coaching_jobs.cfm

About becoming a Life Coach
www.lifecoach.com

Additional Reading
Brown-Volkman, Deborah. *Four Steps to Building a Profitable Coaching Practice: A Complete Marketing Resource for Coaches* (iUniverse, 2003).

Flaherty, James. *Coaching: Evoking Excellence in Others* (Butterworth-Heinemann, 2005).

Sabock, Ralph. *Coaching: A Realistic Perspective* (Rowman and Littlefield Publishers, 2008).

Stanton, Carol and Katy Dockril. *Life Coach in a Box: A Motivational Kit for Making the Most out of Life* (Chronicle Books, 2006).

Williams, Patrick and Diane Menendez. *Becoming a Professional Life Coach: Lessons from the Institute of Life Coach Training* (W.W. Norton and Co., 2007).

CHAPTER SEVEN

FINDING OPPORTUNITIES
IN ADMINISTRATION

If you were in teaching for very long, it is likely that you ran into at least one principal or other administrator who caused you to mutter to yourself, "I could do that job so much better." Perhaps you might pursue that thought now and stay in the public school system, only this time from the administrative side as a principal or assistant principal.

Making the Transition

Being a principal keeps you involved in the public or private school system (unless you choose another venue), but from a radically different perspective. Here are some questions to ask yourself when pondering this direction.

What Kind of Experiences Have You Had with the Principals and/or Assistant Principals Where You Have Worked?

Your perspective on what a principal does might be colored by whether you've had positive or negative experiences within your employment. It is easy to think you could do a better job if you don't realize all that the job entails. Put all your opinions aside for a moment and explore what a principal's job involves before setting your sights on this position.

Would You Have Difficulty Exercising Authority over Teachers after Having Been One Yourself?

This might not be a problem for you at all—but it might be, especially if you get a job in the same school system where you worked before. Having authority over former peers can be touchy, so you might want to choose another school or be prepared to tackle the issue head-on once you are hired.

How Much Experience Have You Had Overseeing the Jobs of a Number of People?

Have you ever had a job where a dozen or more people report to you? If not, it can be rather intimidating at first. Principals typically are involved with all aspects of their schools and even though they have a staff to turn to for assistance, it can still seem quite overwhelming if it's a new situation for you.

Where Would You Ideally Like to Be a Principal?

Although more than half of all principals work in public and private elementary and secondary schools, these systems are not the only ones available. Principals are also employed at preschools, day care centers, universities and colleges, and educational programs such as businesses, correctional institutions, museums, and community organizations. Each one has its own advantages and disadvantages, of course, so you need to do some research to find out what is available in your area and what the requirements are for each one.

Do You Think You Would Prefer a Principal or Assistant Principal Position?

The responsibilities for each job are similar, but different. Naturally, the principal has more overall duties and

"Whatever path someone takes to become an administrator— whether it is through the teaching ranks or from outside of education, whether someone has had years of teaching experience or none—there is a new adventure waiting. Administration is a rare opportunity to marry leadership and followership, creativity and redundancy, and scholar and manager."

—Jane Sigford,
Who Said School Administration Would Be Fun?

makes more money. However, the job also tends to bring more stress. The assistant principal job also requires less education or certification. You have to weigh the pros and cons. Of course, not all schools even have assistant principal jobs; it depends on the size of the school and its enrollment.

The job of principal is one that requires someone who can multitask well—and know when and to whom to delegate. Typical responsibilities include:

- establishing and maintaining contact with students and their families
- acting as liaison between the school and the community
- setting educational goals and standards for the school
- establishing and enforcing policies and procedures
- supervising the school staff, including teachers, counselors, librarians, coaches, and janitorial
- monitoring students' progress
- hiring, firing, and training teachers
- preparing budgets and reports
- keeping detailed records and files
- developing mission statements for the school
- creating unique student programs
- advising, explaining, and answering questions for the staff
- examining learning materials
- visiting classrooms
- watching teaching methods
- interacting with other administrators

- representing the school to other organizations
- fundraising for the school
- ensuring that the school meets national, state, and local standards

Assistant principals often take care of some of the tasks listed above, as well as:

- scheduling student classes
- ordering textbooks and other supplies
- coordinating the details of student transportation
- working with the custodial and cafeteria staff
- creating social and recreational programs for students
- overseeing resources for student health and safety

Do you need additional education in order to be a principal? It depends on your level of education and the school's requirements. Some teachers go directly from the classroom to being either an assistant principal or principal. Some return to school first to get their master's or even a doctoral degree in educational administration or educational leadership. If you choose to work at a preschool or child-care center, you most likely can qualify with just your teaching degree.

A degree in educational administration can be obtained through many schools and, increasingly, online. The course includes classes on the fundamentals of school leadership, educational administrative principles, curriculum design, school law, principles of supervision, diversity issues, and funding. It is hard to predict how long it would take you to complete the program since it would depend on whether you went full- or part-time, in person or online, and for a master's or doctoral degree. Some schools known for educational administration degrees include:

"There is nothing that prepares one better for school administration than teaching. The skills and talents developed and refined as a veteran teacher are not lost when one becomes a school administrator. One becomes a better administrator as a result."

—Rueben Mirabal, Personnel Specialist, http://www .education.org/ career-guidance/ school-administrators .html

- University of Phoenix
- Argosy University
- Kaplan University
- Walden University
- New England College
- University of Cincinnati

You can find many resources for obtaining this degree at http://www.gradschools.com/Subject/Educational-Administration/103.html.

"Administration is a great experience that has a new day involved with it every time you go to work. . . . In this field there is something to do every minute of the day. As an administrator, you may as well say goodbye to conference periods, lunch periods and leaving right after school. Always remember your teaching experience can be very useful when moving to administration. There is no better experience than when you experience the good and bad administrators you have in your career."

—Frank Zavala, *My First Year of School Administration*

Compensation

Statistics show that jobs for school administrators will remain steady from now through the next decade. Salaries depend on the level of school but average:

Principal

senior high	$92,965
junior high	87,866
elementary	82,414

Assistant Principal

senior high	$75,121
junior high	73,020
elementary	67,735

Being behind the administrative desk instead of the teacher's desk may feel just right to you—or very wrong. You may miss the one-on-one interaction with the students. You will still spend time with them, but you won't be teaching as much as disciplining. You may also have trouble acting as the boss of your former coworkers and colleagues. Conflicts with others within the administration are fairly common; if you don't deal well with confrontation, this may be a difficult position to hold. The job involves an endless number of meetings as well, so patience and the ability to listen well will be high priorities.

Becoming a principal is one of the best ways to stay part of the public school system—if, indeed, that is what you want to do with your career. You can utilize many skills you learned in the classroom, but have even more impact on the lives of other teachers and countless students.

"A principal's day can be full of excitement, pressure, conflict, intensity, pathos, joy, sadness, confusion and order. To keep on an even keel, principals must know who they are, what they believe, and what the limits and the license of their job are. Whether alone or with one or more assistants, the principal is responsible for the various aspects of managing a school: planning; scheduling; developing programs and curriculum; supervising personnel; student activities, and student behavior; providing instructional leadership; and fostering professional development."
—Roy Edelfelt and Alan Reiman, *Careers in Education*

Interested in this field? Consider these questions and think about how the answers might affect this career choice:

1. How are you at multitasking?

2. Do you have any trouble delegating tasks so that you are not overwhelmed?

3. Are you willing to get additional education in order to quality for an administrative job?

4. Do you want to be the person in charge or the assistant in charge?

5. Are you interested in going higher up and getting a job as principal (referred to often as provost) at a local college or university?

6. Are you willing to take on a job that will almost certainly involve long hours as well as before and after school activities?

7. Are you comfortable in front of audiences? This job typically entails giving presentations to local organizations and groups.

8. Being a principal means maintaining a certain image in public. Are you comfortable with this?

9. Do you know your state's educational guidelines? Can you create a school that fits them, as well as federal and local standards?

10. Do you like holding a position where everyone will turn to you for decisions and guidance?

Further Resources to Investigate

Organizations
The National Association of Elementary School Principals
1615 Duke Street
Alexandria, VA 22314-3483
www.neasp.org

The National Association of Secondary School Principals
1904 Association Drive
Reston, VA 20191-1537
www.nassp.org

American Association of School Administrators
801 N. Quincy Street
Suite 700
Arlington, VA 22203-1730
www.aasa.org

American Association of University Administrators
P.O. Box 630101
Little Neck, NY 11363
www.aaua.org

Website
The American Association of School Administrators
www.aasa.org

Additional Reading
Gorton, Richard, and July Alston. *School Leadership and Administration: Important Concepts, Case Studies and Simulations* (McGraw-Hill Humanities/Social Sciences/Languages, 2008).

Hall, Charles. *So You Want to be a School Administrator? The Sure Fire Way to Land that Principal or Superintendent Job* (iUniverse, 2000).

CHAPTER EIGHT

ENRICHMENT TEACHING

Perhaps you are ready for a change—but not a huge change. Maybe you want to leave behind the No Child Left Behind rules and regulations. Maybe you are ready to teach students subjects they are sincerely interested in, not to improve their overall GPAs or college prep transcripts, but to improve their lives in some way. Does that sound like you? If so, you might investigate becoming a teacher who specializes in what are known as self-enrichment classes. All that you need for these types of classes, which are considered non-academic, is enthusiasm and experience. No license or other formal education is typically required.

Is Specialized Teaching for You?

To find out if these types of classes might be a potential avenue for you, consider these questions.

What Types of Classes Would You Be Interested in Teaching if You Could Choose Absolutely Any Subject?

To answer this question, you should probably write out a list similar to the one you considered when thinking about tutoring or coaching. However, here you need to really look beyond the academic box that you are used to remaining within. Think about your hobbies, preferences, talents, former jobs/careers, and so on. What can you come up with?

Could You Easily Adapt to Teaching Classes That Might Only Last for a Short Period of Time Rather Than the Typical 8 to 3 School Day?

Some of the classes you might teach may meet once for a long period of time, or maybe once a week, or in some other odd configuration. This will, on one hand, give you a great deal more free time when you're not teaching, but it will also mean less money, depending on how many different classes you might be teaching.

Are You Comfortable Working with Small Groups Rather Than Large Classrooms? How Well Do You Deal with One-on-One Instruction?

Many non-academic classes are going to be small, with perhaps a handful (four to six) of students instead of a full classroom of 30 or more. In many ways, this is beneficial, as you will have a far better chance to give the students individual attention and guidance, plus get to know their personalities, their learning styles, and their learning paces much more thoroughly. Discipline issues are usually much rarer in this type of setting. Since these students have paid to take the class, they are typically a great deal more interested and attentive to what you are teaching than the typical public school student may be. You may also find that you want to meet with these students one-on-one occasionally for some extra instruction or assistance since you know them on a more intense academic level. Being comfortable within this situation is vital.

How Do You Feel about Working with Students on a Life Skill Rather Than an Academic Subject?

The topics you typically cover as a self-enrichment teacher are a long way from the reading, writing, and arithmetic classes of public and private school. For some, this means a real sense of freedom and the chance to do whatever feels right without having to go through the red tape of administrative and/or parental approval first. For others, this freedom may feel intimidating and make you insecure.

Are You All Right Leaving the Whole A-B-C Grade Scale Behind?

Many self-enrichment classes have no grading whatsoever, only a casual pass/fail attitude or, more likely, the simple satisfaction of learning how to make or do something new. The days of A, B, and Cs and a strict obsession with GPAs are probably not on the radar, at least for now. Are you comfortable with that? Are you familiar with other ways to grade or judge a student's performance?

Are You Willing to Work on Weekends and Weeknights Instead of During the Day?

You will be offering classes to people who probably already go to school and/or work full-time, so their free time is quite limited. Most of your classes will be squeezed into hours like mid to late evening or throughout the weekend. Are you willing to give up that time to teach? Which do you prefer?

Do You Know How Much Your Time and Expertise Is Worth?

How much to charge for your classes will depend on many different factors: your location, the competition, your experience level, the length and number of sessions, the materials needed or provided, and how much you

"Ever since I was a little girl, I've known this is my gift: to help others feel good about themselves, to increase their self-esteem and self-confidence.... The best part of my job is seeing someone blossom."
—Lori Johnson, Image Consultant

personally feel your time and effort is worth. Go online and see if there are others teaching similar classes. How much are they charging? Check out the national levels, if possible, and then carefully compare.

How Experienced Are You with Self-Promotion and Marketing?

Just as with any self-employment position, you will largely be responsible for your own promotion and marketing. You can print up business cards, post fliers, send out brochures, give interviews to prospective students and parents, and much more. How much you do is governed by your time constraints as well as your personal comfort levels.

Just As You Had to Consider with Tutoring, Do You Want to Teach Classes in Your Home or at a Separate Site?

Much of this answer will depend on what you are teaching and how many students you have at any one time. It will also depend on whether you are working for yourself or teaching a community class through a local college or other organization.

Topics to Consider

What kind of self-enrichment classes could you teach? Make a list of topics in which you feel you have expertise. Then, you could put the results in several categories. For example, you could arrange them from the classes you would most like to teach to the ones you would least like to. You could put them in the order of how well you know each one—could you teach a beginning, moderate, or advanced level course? Just remember to look beyond what you've covered in your classroom classes to more personal subjects. Here is a list of possibilities that might inspire you. What else can you think of?

photography
pottery
cooking or baking
personal finance
time management
yoga
dancing
singing
painting/sculpting/carving
creative writing
musical instrument
kayaking
knitting
gardening
calligraphy
drawing/sketching
glass art
jewelry art
drama
graphic arts
wine appreciation
horticulture
flower arranging
sewing
wood crafts

home improvement
interior decorating
upholstery
pet care
foreign language
quilting
American Sign Language
test preparation
world religions
fashion design
accounting
computer care and
troubleshooting
home buying
real estate investing
dating and relationships
herbal medicine
meditation
automotive care
job preparation (interviewing,
    writing resumes, etc.)
hiking and camping skills
marriage preparation
literacy or ESL tutoring

Changing Your Typical Class Structure

Many skills you used in the classroom will be put to work in self-enrichment classes as well. You will still need to develop lesson plans. Depending on the topic, you may have to adjust how much time you spend lecturing as opposed conducting to hands-on lessons and demonstrations. Instead of homework assignments, you will most likely encourage your students to work on projects (either during class, in their free time, or both) or do some reading in preparation for the next meeting. Since these classes are voluntary for students, the only ones to pay the price for not doing the work are the students themselves; there are no report cards or GPAs.

How long each course is depends on what you plan to teach. For example, you might teach one afternoon class on how to use beads to make a necklace, or you could teach a month-long course on sewing, taking students from pattern and material to a finished, wearable project. You could have a two-week course on baking bread or a six-month course on Mediterranean dishes. Other lessons, such as playing musical instruments, singing, and other arts, can go on as long as you and the students want them to, as there is always something more to learn.

The Downsides

The downsides of this job are almost the same as with tutoring—many times, students will fail to show up or do their projects because this isn't considered a real class with real grades and real consequences. Many times, classes won't even get off the ground because not enough people sign up, even though you have done all the prep work. People will not pay you when and what they are supposed to. You might get burned out on teaching again. All of these are possibilities to be aware of before making any final decisions about a career change to this new type of teaching.

Compensation

Statistics show that this field is going to grow at a much faster than average speed through 2016. A growing number of adult learners are interested in developing new skills and pursuing new interests, and that means they need teachers. The average income for these teachers was

"Look at what you are planning to teach with the geographic area around you in mind. Are there other teachers of the same subject? Is it because the subject is popular and there is plenty of room for more teachers in this area? Why is no one else teaching your topic? Is it because there is no interest or is the interest there but there are no teachers with the appropriate knowledge? Are there enough children in your area in the age range you want to teach?"
—Stephanie Quinn, *Start a Business Teaching Kids*

$16.08 an hour in 2006. Typically, self-enrichment class teachers are paid by the hour.

Interested in this field? Consider these questions and think about how the answers might affect this career choice:

1. Are you comfortable charging for your services and then doing the necessary paperwork to collect and apply the fees?

2. Are there community colleges and other organizations in your area that need teachers for their nonacademic courses?

3. Are you able to multitask enough to teach a variety of different classes at the same time?

4. How close to academic subjects do you want to stick? Are you more comfortable with teaching accounting tips than flirting techniques?

5. What are the top five classes that you would feel comfortable teaching? What do you think the market is for them in your area? Do some research to find out.

6. How many hours do you need to work to secure the income you are hoping for?

7. How many students could you handle at any one time considering the topic you want to pursue most?

8. Are there any colleagues, former students or others that could write testimonials and/or reference letters for you?

9. Can you write and distribute your own advertising with confidence?

10. Is this type of teaching enough of a change to warrant quitting your job or do you want to try and combine it with your full-time job instead?

Teaching may still be your thing, but you just want to change when, how, and with whom you do it. In that case, self-enrichment teaching may be just what you have been looking for.

Further Resources to Investigate

Organizations

The National Enrichment Teachers Association, Inc.
13428 Maxella Avenue, #436
Marina Del Rey, CA 90292
www.netanational.org

The U.S. Department of Education
Office of Adult and Vocational Education
Potomac Center Plaza
400 Maryland Avenue SW
Washington, DC 20202
www.ed.gov/index.jhtml

Association for Career and Technical Education
1410 King Street
Alexandria, VA 22314
www.acteonline.org

Additional Reading

Most titles are going to be found by looking up the topic you are most interested in teaching, rather than an all-encompassing title that addresses self-enrichment classes.

Freedman, Tanya. *Start and Run an Art Teaching Business* (Self-Counsel Press, 2007).

Palmer, Pati. *The Business of Teaching Sewing* (Palmer/Pletsch Publishing, 2007).

Quinn, Stephanie. *Start a Business Teaching Kids* (Quinn Entertainment, 2005).

CHAPTER NINE

TEACHING ABROAD

An ad for this teaching option might read, "See the world! Travel from one end of the planet to the next—and teach students somewhere in the process!" The field of teaching in foreign countries has been around for some time and shows little sign of slowing down. Since English has become a language that people speak all around the world, teachers who are trained and clearly able to show students how to become fluent (and learn a few other things in the process) are constantly in demand. Jobs are typically found in foreign-based American schools, as well as British schools, Department of Defense schools, and both private locally run and nonprofit schools.

Are You Really Ready for an Adventure?

Deciding whether you want to pack your bags and move to the other side of the globe for at least a year (and most likely, more) is a big decision. More than just changing careers, it means being separated from everything that is familiar, including your culture, community, friends, and family. To some this is exciting; to others, it is terrifying. Work through the following questions as you mull it over.

Are There Particular Countries You Would and Would Not Like to Go To?

Is there an area you have always wanted to explore or to avoid? Have these in mind before you start the job search. You cannot be guaranteed only the area you have specified; other areas may offer you a job that you are free to accept or reject.

What Is Your Background in Teaching English Reading, Writing, and Speaking? Do You Have Experience in ESL?

Although you do not usually have to be an English teacher to secure one of these overseas teaching positions, it certainly can give you the edge. If you're a former math teacher, you may have more to prove when you apply to teach English skills. Of course, if you have any ESL training that is also a bonus.

Are You Single or Married? Will Your Spouse/Partner Be Going with You?

Some schools will allow teachers to bring along a spouse, although most prefer single teachers. If you are married, a long separation may be a real complication and a major factor to consider.

What Foreign Languages, if Any, Do You Speak Already?

Do you already know Spanish, Italian, French, German, or Japanese? If you do, that's a definite plus. If you know a foreign language but it has been years since you used it, consider picking up a textbook or CD or taking a course to brush up on your skills.

"Although our lives have been very ordinary in one sense, they have been filled with adventure and new learning every day. Both our girls . . . were born overseas. Our best friendships have come from the ranks of teachers who've chosen this life, even for a brief time, Our girls speak several languages and easily navigate around the world, as that has been their world."

—Karen Dunmire, international teacher, and principal of the American School in Warsaw, Poland

How Good Are You at Adapting to Different Cultures, Habits, and Mannerisms?

Flexibility is essential in order to succeed in this venture. Keep in mind that when you go to another country, you are the foreigner who has to adapt to a great many changes. As soon as you find out which country you are going to, it is highly recommended that you study books about its culture so you can be familiar with slang, gestures, and other methods of communication, as well as general styles of living.

Ideally, How Long Would You Like to Be Gone?

Each school is different but typically overseas teaching contracts are for at least one year and usually two. Just like in the United States, foreign schools tend to start their school years in September and you will need to do your traveling in August. Hiring takes place in May or June, so you will have plenty of time to prepare.

How Much Traveling Experience Have You Had?

Are you familiar with finding the right airport gates, grabbing your luggage off at the baggage claim, hailing a taxi, and all the other elements involved in traveling? That will help with making the transition from one country to another smoothly.

Do You Have All the Qualifications for Teaching Overseas?

- You speak English at a native level.
- You have strong familiarity with Western curricula.

- You have strong teaching abilities.
- You have at least two years of teaching experience.
- You have a bachelor's degree.
- You have a teacher's certification.
- You possess flexibility in your personal and professional life.
- You have an ability to convey enthusiasm.
- You have a minimum of two-year availability.
- You are able to get strong references.

While these qualifications are considered requirements, other factors are a plus, including:

- experience living overseas
- dedication to multiculturalism
- a strong background in extracurricular activities
- knowledge of foreign languages

"Learn a new language, cook authentic local food, try some kangaroo meat, help build a home for a refugee family . . . these are one of a kind experiences that open up new horizons and broaden an individual's perspective on the world."
—www.educator overseas.com

Compensation

One of the biggest perks to teaching overseas, obviously, is that you get the chance to experience another way of life and culture up close and personal. You will get to explore parts of the world you may not have gotten the chance to see otherwise. Teaching abroad may easily give you some of the most exotic and memorable moments of your life.

How much you will be paid varies from country to country, school to school. Obviously, if you end up teaching in a very expensive, well-known city like London or Paris, you will use up a great deal of your salary on daily expenses as the standard of living is quite high. On the other hand, if you choose a job in a smaller, lesser known area of the world, you will be much more likely to afford it and have some left over for saving at the end of each month.

What do these schools pay for? Again, it depends on the school and the country, but typically the costs covered include:

- airfare to and from the city where you will be teaching

- health insurance

- housing

- summer vacations

- help with learning the country's language

- assistance with getting any necessary paperwork like visas and permits

In addition, some schools also supply a vehicle for personal use, a shopping allowance for basic needs, and a computer. Some will even give you a retirement plan and life insurance.

"Recruiters are only going to employ people who they judge to be able to thrive in challenging environments and in the midst of culture shock. It's fine to suffer from culture shock, but you must be able to function in your job whilst going through the shock of moving countries. . . . It's tough enough learning your way around a new city in your own home country, now imagine going through that learning process in a different country where you don't speak the language and can't read any of the signs. If this sounds awful to you, rather than an exciting opportunity, then you probably aren't the right person for a position at an international school. There are lots of opportunities for you to work in a country more in line with what you're used to."

—Kelly Blackwell, "Teaching Overseas: Are You the Right Person for the Job?"

Taking Precautions

If you're ready to sign on the dotted line and toss your bags on the airplane, take a deep breath and do just a little bit more homework. It's a sad but true fact that there are countless scams and con artists in the world—and when it comes to overseas jobs, there can be quite a few of them. They prey on your sense of adventure, hoping that your excitement over the job will overrule your intuition or good sense. The Federal Trade Commission and the Better Business Bureau are both aware of overseas scams and they have some good advice for you. The FTC says to watch for these tell-tale signs:

- They ask for money up front.
- They use post office boxes instead of office street addresses.
- They make promises of employment and guarantees of refunds.
- They charge fees for giving you a job lead.
- They have 900-number operators.

To show what some unscrupulous companies can do, the BBB tells the story of a consumer who answered an ad telling applicants to call an 800 toll-free number for more information. When the person did, he heard a recording directing him to call a 900 number to find out what job openings were available. At this number, however, the applicant was told to send a self-addressed, stamped envelope to an address and an application would be sent in the mail. The consumer did so and received a generic one-page job application—and a $39 charge on his phone bill.

To keep yourself safe from scams, both the FTC and BBB offer the following recommendations:

- You should ask for references.
- Check them out in the state they list as an address.

- Get everything in writing.

- Forget about companies with no legitimate street address.

- Be very skeptical of overseas employment opportunities that sound too good to be true.

- Never send cash in the mail, and be extremely cautious with firms that require a money order. This could indicate that the firm is attempting to avoid a traceable record of its transactions.

- Do not be fooled by official-sounding names. Many scam artists operate under names that sound like those of long-standing, reputable firms.

- Avoid working with firms that require payment in advance.

- Do not give your credit card or bank account number to telephone solicitors.

- Read the contract very carefully. Have an attorney look over any documents you are asked to sign.

- Beware of an agency that is unwilling to give you a written contract.

- Do not hesitate to ask questions. You have a right to know what services to expect and the costs involved. For example, ask how long the company has been in business.

- Do not make a hasty decision. Instead, take time to weigh all the pros and cons of the situation. Be wary of demands that "You must act now."

- Keep a copy of all agreements you sign, as well as copies of checks you forward to the company.

- Check with the embassy of the country where the job is supposed to be located. Make sure you are eligible to work there.

- If the firm has a refund policy, ask for specific written details and read the fine print.

One common scam is to include a requirement that job seekers check in routinely with the firm—at their own expense, of course. Those who do not do so lose their opportunity for a refund and they aren't told this fact until they ask.

There is little doubt that deciding to teach in a foreign country is an alluring idea. Who doesn't want to see exotic places in the world, eat new foods, discover new ways of life, and meet new friends? However, a commitment like this one is not the same as a two-week vacation spent sightseeing. This is work. You will have many of the same situations and demands wherever you go as you had in your American classroom—except now you will be thousands of miles from home. Think long and hard and then if you decide to go, bon voyage!

"Some unfortunate job seekers have been instructed to meet at a particular place to fly to their new jobs, only to find no airline tickets, no job, and often, no more company."
—Better Business Bureau

Interested in this field? Consider these questions and think about how the answers might affect this career choice:

1. Do you have an up-to-date passport? Do you know how and where to get one?

2. Are there any immunizations you will need to go to another country? Are you willing to get them?

3. Do you have any religious or cultural beliefs that might clash in another culture?

4. Are you a certified teacher? In case you are not, go to the American Board for Certification of Teacher Excellence (www.abcte.org) for information and assistance.

5. Are you more interested in teaching in large, well-known countries like Spain, Italy, China, or the U.K. or in smaller, lesser known countries like Romania, Guam, Albania, or Sri Lanka?

6. Do you have a savings account or backup income in case you need extra money while overseas?

7. Who, if anyone, would come to this new country with you? How do he, she, or they feel about the whole idea?

8. Do you have time to look for a job overseas? It is not a quick search. The experts say it can take an average of 6 to 12 months to find the right job. Are you in a hurry?

9. Is your resume appropriate for using on an international basis? Resumes designed for American employers to read may differ significantly from those sent to other countries to be read. Mary Anne Thompson, author of *The Global Resume and CV Guide*, recommends, "The best advice is to do your homework—find out what's appropriate according to the corporate culture, the country culture, and the culture of the person making the hiring decision. The challenge will be to incorporate these different cultures in one document," she adds. (For more about how to design your resume, you can check out Thompson's article at http://www .overseasdigest.com/globalcv.htm.)

10. Do you generally stick to the commitments you make? Teaching abroad is a large decision—and once you are overseas, it is complicated to change your mind and end your contract.

"I found out why teachers rarely go back to teaching in the United States after teaching abroad. Where else can one be paid to hike a volcano, snorkel beautiful coral reefs, or learn about survival deep in the jungle?"
—*Bill Jordan, international teacher*

Further Resources to Investigate

Organization
Office of Overseas Schools
U.S. Department of State
Room H328 SA-1
Washington, DC 20522-0132

Websites
Teaching Abroad
http://www.teachingabroad.net/

Overseas Digest
http://www.overseasdigest.com/

Department of Defense Overseas Schools
www.dodea.edu

Friends of World Teaching
www.fowt.com

Additional Reading
Griffith, Susan. *Teaching English Abroad* (Vacation Work Publications, 2007).

Hayden, Mary. *Introduction to International Education: International Schools and their Communities* (Sage Publications, 2006).

Slethaug, Gordon E. *Teaching Abroad: International Education and the Cross-Cultural Classroom* (Hong Kong University Press, 2007).

CHAPTER TEN

TEACHING ONLINE

It sometimes seems like computers have taken over the world, just like sneaky robots do in science fiction novels and movies. At first they seem helpful, but before you know it, they are vying for world domination.

Although in reality computers are not maniacal pieces of electronics out to take over the planet, they have impacted our culture in endless ways. They have made going to the library, walking out to the mailbox, or turning on your television options rather than a regular occurrence. In the world of education, **distance learning**, as it has come to be known, has also had a huge impact. (It is also sometimes referred to as **distributed learning** or **remote education**.) According to the National Center for Education Statistics and other reliable resources:

- During the 2006–2007 academic year, 66 percent of U.S. two-year and four-year postsecondary institutions offered college-level online education sources. Since then, that number has grown to 80 percent.

- The most common reasons that institutions offer distance learning are: meeting student demand for flexible schedules, providing access to college for students who would otherwise not have access, making more courses available, and seeking to increase student enrollment.

- In the 2006–2007 academic year, 12.2 million students were enrolled in college-level, credit-granting distance learning courses.

Is Virtual Teaching for You?

All of these students taking all of these courses mean one thing for you: a job, if you are comfortable and savvy enough with computers to be a distance educator. Does that sound just like you? Think through a few questions.

How Much Do You Know How to Do on a Computer?

While you don't have to be a techno geek to be a distance educator, you will need a decent understanding of how your computer works and the basic troubleshooting techniques to use if/when you encounter a problem. Since your entire class interaction will be conducted through your computer, it has to be in tip-top shape. That leads to the next question.

What kind of Computer System Do You Have to Use Daily?

Teaching online courses means having a computer that can handle all that you ask of it, including downloading and uploading different materials. Investing money to ensure you have a good amount of memory, a decent video card, and, of course, a writing program like Microsoft Word is essential. Familiarity with various programs like Excel, Adobe, and PhotoShop are often necessary, as well. You have to have a computer that can move fast enough to keep up, because a slow-moving one will only frustrate you and increase the time you have to spend in front of the screen.

How Much Time Do You Want to Spend on a Computer on a Daily Basis?

On the average, how much time do you spend on the computer each day? If you're used to only checking your e-mail, reading the online news, and then turning the computer off, it might be hard for you to adjust to the time you will need to spend online to prepare and monitor your classes. If your normal teaching day has you being extremely physically active, you might want to give this some extra thought. You can still teach the distance courses, but you may have to bump up your time at the gym to make up for the time spent sitting at the computer.

How Good Are Your Writing Skills?

Unlike in the typical classroom setting, with an online course you may not be able to rely on lecturing to teach material. In these cases, you will have to rely far more on your writing skills as you write out your lessons, homework assignments, and other activities. For some teachers, this will feel quite familiar; for others who have depended on lecturing in order to get information across, this new skill set can be a challenge to learn and use. As technology continues to evolve, however, this will likely change. For example, the technique of webcasting, or broadcasting across the web, gives a person the ability to transmit a live presentation over the Internet to an unlimited audience.

Have You Ever Taken an Online Course?

Personal experience will help you to better understand how to be a good online teacher—take a course and see the online learning process from the perspective of a student. Even if it is a brief class, take one and then pay close attention to what the instructor does well—and what he or she does not. Observation will help guide you

"In the future, as costs decrease . . . , you will find people using web casting for everything from online family reunions and sales presentations, to home-based cooking shows and pay per view seminars. As the technology improves, the potential use will skyrocket."

—Jim Edwards, TheNetReporter .com columnist

to how you want to teach your courses. Is your instructor easy to access? Does she respond quickly to questions? How does he collect assignments? What does she do to keep the course interesting? These are all lessons for you on what to do and not do when you move into the role of instructor.

How Skilled Are You at Self-Discipline and Time Management?

Just as online courses give you freedom, they also give you more responsibility; you have to be sure you keep up-to-date without anyone actually looking over your shoulder to remind you of your day-to-day responsibilities. It has been shown that students are far more likely to complete an online course if their teachers are prompt with their feedback. It is essential that you are able to keep up with homework assignments, papers, quizzes, and lesson plans. Many distance courses also feature discussion forums or boards that you may play a part in and/or have to monitor on a regular basis.

What Level Classes Are You Able and Interested in Teaching?

Although the majority of distance learning courses are college-level, not all of them are. A growing number of classes for the younger grades are also being offered thanks to the growth of educational alternatives like virtual high schools, homebound students, and homeschooling. High school and even lower-grade courses are being offered to a number of students throughout the country. Are you able to teach these grades? Which ones are you most comfortable with?

Do You Know How to Upload Video and/or Audio Clips from the Internet?

You will need to be fairly computer savvy in order to teach an online course. These classes are interactive, which, as you know from being in the classroom, means actively involving the student in as many ways as possible from reading and writing to listening and watching. Often this can involve uploading a variety of materials from the Internet.

Are You Good at Facilitating Student Discussions Online?

Discussion forums are, as mentioned earlier, a common element in online courses. It gives students the chance to talk with each other about different aspects of the class and it gives you, as the teacher, a chance to read their thoughts, perspectives, opinions, and so on. Many times, the instructor does little more than provide the discussion topic and require responses as part of the course requirements and then keep an eye on the forum. Other times, the instructor may participate in the forum with comments and ideas as well, especially if the conversations seem to stall or go in the wrong direction.

Can You Deal with Working with Students Whom You Likely Will Never See Face-To-Face?

Almost all distance learning courses you teach will be designed so that your students come from around the country, so you won't get the chance to actually meet them face-to-face. Are you comfortable with that? You won't be able to watch them to get a sense of their levels of understanding, their personalities, their learning styles, and so on. You will have to rely on their assignments, e-mails, and other electronic communications to figure these things out.

What Else You Can Expect

Distance learning is a great opportunity for both students and teachers. It often helps students save time and money. They can learn at the privacy of their own computers, rather in a room full of their peers where the competition is often much higher. At the same time, it gives you the space and time to focus on ideas, enrichment activities, and other curricula that you wouldn't have the chance to consider when working with multiple classrooms comprised of 30 students or more. Distance learning also provides for far greater flexibility as you and your student or students can work at the time that is most convenient. If either of you are night owls, that's fine. If you are up the second the sun clears the horizon that works, too. If you have far more time on Tuesdays and Thursdays than on the other days of the week, great. Distance learning gives everyone involved the ability to design their own schedules.

> *"The instructor's role in the online course is different than that of a classroom teacher. It is just as vital to the movement of students toward achieving learning goals, but in different ways. Perhaps to a greater degree than the traditional classroom, the online environment allows the instructor to model the behavior of a learner for his or her students. Carroll suggests that we are moving toward new learning environments where there are no teachers and no students, only learners. If this is so, perhaps my greatest stumbling block as an online instructor newbie was the unconscious, instinctive tendency to teach as I had been taught."*
> —Bobby Hobgood, online teacher

Of course, don't let extra flexibility lull you into a false sense of security about deadlines. You will still have due dates your students need to adhere to—they just have more freedom as to when they work to meet that deadline, just as you have more as to when you will look at what they have turned in.

Some of these distance education courses are synchronous, which means that you and your students interact with each other in what is referred to as "real time," such as in videoconferencing, telephone calls, and Internet chat programs. Other courses are asynchronous, which means there is a delay in the student/ teacher interaction. This includes methods such as videotape, audiotape, and e-mail.

The majority of distance educators' jobs are through an established school or institution, which typically pays per course. Some distance educators who specialize in non-academic courses work freelance instead, and charge whatever the going rate is for the region.

Challenges of Online Education

Online teaching is a fabulous field to get into, but it will call on some of your best teaching skills. How do you motivate the student who you can't see face-to-face? How do you involve him when he is sitting in front of a computer screen instead of in the classroom with you? It can be quite challenging. It can also be quite enjoyable and a way to make money spending the day exploring and using a computer.

Interested in this field? Consider these questions and think about how the answers might affect this career choice.

1. What is your attitude about the quality of online learning courses?

2. Are you used to checking your e-mail on a frequent basis? Do you respond quickly?

3. Do you enjoy being on the computer?

4. What types of teaching methods do you have experience with other than lecturing?

5. How savvy are you on different computer software programs?

6. Do you know how to work with technology such as podcasting and webcasting?

7. What ideas do you have about keeping long distance students motivated and involved?

8. Have you had experience with discussion forums? Are you comfortable with them?

9. Do you have the equipment you need for distance learning (computer, phone, fax machine, copier, scanner, etc.) or will the learning institute provide it?

10. Would you prefer synchronous or asynchronous courses and why?

"Do you remember a time when you gave the wrong answer in class? When people may have laughed or made faces, or even made comments to you later? That kind of negative reinforcement didn't make you want to participate much the next time a class discussion rolled around. And you probably had to give that answer quickly—the classroom often doesn't give you a lot of time to think before you have to give an answer. Or what if you had the right answer? You might have still gotten laughter or dirty looks for being an egghead or a nerd. You may have refrained from talking the next time, or dumbed down your answer. In an online course, you are free to research, to think, and to edit before you post your comments. You won't hear any immediate response, so while it may be a while before anyone answers, you won't get any laughter or dirty looks. You're more likely to get a well-reasoned, well-researched response from a classmate or instructor."
—Ross White, Director of Online Learning, Learn NC

Further Resources to Investigate

Organization
You can find jobs and associated information at:
SUNY Learning Network, http://www.geteducated.com/online-education-careers/13-online-education-careers/96-online-and-distance-job-postings.

Additional Reading

Finkelstein, Jonathan E. *Learning in Real Time: Synchronous Teaching and Learning Online* (Jossey-Bass, 2006).

Levine, S. Joseph. *"Making Distance Education Work: Understanding Learning and Learners at a Distance"* (Lulu.com, 2005).

Simonson, Michael. *Teaching and Learning at a Distance: Foundations of Distance Education* (Prentice-Hall, 2008).

SECTION II

So, Now What?

The first portion of this book was dedicated to thoroughly exploring the many different career options that exist for anyone with a teaching degree. Hopefully, it helped you pinpoint some possibilities that intrigued you enough to do some more studying and research for yourself.

The rest of the book focuses on the actual job process, from finding out where to search for jobs and how to apply to them properly to how to ace the interview and say a polite and effective goodbye to your current teaching career. Good luck!

CHAPTER ELEVEN

CREATING A WINNING RESUME AND COVER LETTER

There is little doubt that a well done, professional resume or CV and cover letter are important. In most instances, they act as your first contact with an employer and provide your first impression. For that reason alone, you want to make sure that they are well done and represent you at your very best—as well as most hireable!

There are entire books out there that are about nothing other than how to write a great resume. Leafing through a few of them could be quite helpful, as well as searching online for examples. It is helpful to concentrate on resumes that are specifically written by people who are changing careers.

What Makes a Winning Cover Letter?

A cover letter is like a handshake: It says hello, this is who I am, and then briefly conveys a little about you. Just as you don't want your handshake to be weak or clammy, you don't want your cover letter to be unimpressive and forgettable. Cover letters are more powerful than most people may give them credit for. For many busy employers, it is easier to scan the resume quickly but read the cover letter from beginning to end because of its brevity. So make the most out of that single page.

Here are some of the best tips for creating a strong cover letter:

"Your letter should be not only fairly short, but also concise and pithy. Edit your letter mercilessly. Follow the journalist's credo: Write tight! Cut out all unnecessary words and jargon. Then go back and do it again."

—Katharine Hansen, PhD, author of *Dynamic Cover Letters for New Graduates*

1. **"To Whom It May Concern"** is not the way to start your letter. It is far better for you to address it to the person who will be doing the hiring. You may have to call ahead or do some research to locate the right name, but it is worth the effort.

2. **The shorter, the better.** Make sure your cover letter is not more than one page long. Be precise, concise, and focused.

3. **Choose wisely** what words (especially verbs) you use in your letter. You want specific words that clearly paint a portrait of who you are and what you are capable of. Take note—this is what you want to do on your resume, as well. So when you choose those words, pick the ones for the resume as well. Check out the list of power verbs. How many of them can you apply to things you have accomplished?

4. **Speak positively.** End your letter on an up beat with something along the lines of, "I look forward to hearing from you" or "I hope that we can arrange an interview soon."

5. **Ask not what the employer can do for you.** Demonstrate what you can do to help the company rather than what they could or should do for you.

6. **Maintain perfection to the greatest possible extent.** There is absolutely no room in your letter for typos, misspellings, or incorrect grammar or punctuation. Have someone proofread it for you before you send it so you know it's completely error-free.

7. **Only originals, please.** Never make a copy of your last cover letter and use it again. An original should be sent to each potential employer.

8. **Be as interesting as possible.** A boring cover letter is certain to make the wrong impression, so do your best to make yours unique and interesting so the employers will remember it. Don't take this idea to mean, however, that you should use neon colored paper, an odd font, or smiley faces all over your letter and/or resume. Stay professional.

Power Verbs

administered	forecast	proposed
allocated	formulated	recruited
assessed	generated	rehabilitated
broadened	guided	researched
cataloged	handled	revised
chaired	implemented	scheduled
communicated	initiated	specified
coordinated	innovated	staffed
crafted	instituted	streamlined
delegated	launched	transformed
designed	mediated	trimmed
devised	motivated	unified
endorsed	navigated	verified
executed	negotiated	waged
explored	organized	

When you begin writing your cover letter and your resume, you need to target your transferable skills, the ones that can easily be applied to a field other than the field you are leaving. In other words, if you are leaving teaching for a separate field, then you need to summarize your skills in "non-teacherese." Some of the most important skills to highlight include:

- organizational skills
- entrepreneurial skills
- problem-solving skills
- critical thinking
- ability to learn new skills quickly
- ability to multitask
- ability to work under pressure
- ability to meet deadlines
- strong writing skills
- research skills
- ability to get along with a variety of people and cultures

Make a list of the things you have accomplished through your teaching career and then analyze how you can rephrase them to highlight the skills and abilities just listed.

Creating Your Resume

Once your cover letter is ready, it's time to turn to writing the resume itself. There is no blanket resume that will work for every person or every job, of course. Every resume has to be tailored to the specific job description, but here are some general guidelines to keep in mind.

A horrifying fact of job searching is that only one interview is granted for every 200 resumes received. In addition, the average employer only spends 10 to 20 seconds skimming the papers you probably spent hours—or days—putting together. A number of the experts in the field of job hunting encourage job seekers to consider their resume like an advertisement. You are trying to get an employer to "buy" or hire you.

If you start doing some research on how to write an excellent resume, you will quickly discover that everyone has his own take on it. Each advisor or consultant seems to have a great formula; then you get to the next one and it seems just as good. And in all honesty, they probably are all effective because there is no single right style.

Let's take a moment to focus on resumes specifically designed for people changing careers, since that is most likely what you need.

The way you organize your resume is primarily determined by whether you are transitioning to a similar career (classroom teaching to overseas teaching or tutoring) or to something quite different (classroom teaching to publishing). A minimal transition calls for a resume that focuses on your qualifications and certifications, while a bigger change calls for a resume that focuses on your skills while it downplays your work history.

Sample resume formats can be found all over the Internet and in a number of books. A good, basic pattern to use, however would look something like this.

Your Name
Street Address
City, State, Zip
Telephone numbers (landline and cell)
E-mail address

Objective
This is where you list what type of position you are hoping to achieve. Be specific and use strong verbs, as previously listed.

Profile
This is the place to list two to five of your very strongest skills.

Achievements
This is where you list two to four achievements that you accomplished through work, hobbies, education or volunteer work. You might list any awards won and/or civic/community leadership.

Education/Training/Experience
Which one of these you highlight depends on the job you are applying for and what area is strongest in your background. Important professional affiliations could go here as well.

If you are not sure you can create the best possible resume, you can always consider hiring a professional to do so for you.

"An investment in a professionally crafted resume can pay off big time. There's no shame in hiring a professional resume writer. You hire doctors, lawyers, financial advisors, and tax consultants when you lack the expertise in those areas, so why should resume-writing be different? Many employers and even more recruiters actually encourage the idea of professionally written resumes because hiring managers want to obtain your information in a reader-friendly form that clearly tells how you benefit the organization."

—Katharine Hansen, PhD, creative director of
   Quintessential Careers

Here are some other tips for you to keep in mind as you put together your resume:

- Don't put the word "resume" anywhere on it.
- The resume is about you, not about your past employment.
- Keep the job objective to six words or fewer.
- Do not include your personal information or interests.
- Do not include your ethnic or religious affiliations.
- Do not send or attach a photo of yourself unless the specific job application requests it.
- Avoid the use of any professional jargon or slang.
- Don't include "references upon request" or "available for interview" because they are both obvious.

A real quote from a person's resume—who clearly did not get hired. "I got good communicatrion skills and in my previous projects sometimes i handled the project alone.i got some idea in web server administration.i know cold fusion administration. Intrested to relocate anywhere in USA.looking for a better position and iam available right now."

—Taken from http://
www.mekong.
net/tech/resmhits
.htm

Your resume is the toe that gets your foot in the door for a new job. It is a paper model of you and what you have been doing with your life for the past years. If the cover letter is a handshake, then the resume is a quick chat over a cup of coffee. Both of them are designed to secure you the more intense interaction of a face-to-face interview—and then, hopefully, a new job.

Further Resources to Investigate

Organization
Professional Association of Resume Writers and Career Coaches
1388 Brightwaters Boulevard NE
St. Petersburg, FL 33704
http://www.parw.com/contact_parwcc.html

Further Reading
Enelow, Wendy and Louise Kursmark. *Expert Resumes for Career Changers, 3rd edition* (JIST Works, 2010).

Greene, Brenda. *Get the Interview Every Time: Proven Resume and Cover Letter Strategies from Fortune 500 Hiring Professionals* (Kaplan Publishing, 2008).

Levinson, Jay Conrad, et al. *Guerrilla Marketing for Job Hunters 2.0: 1,001 Unconventional Tips, Tricks and Tactics for Landing Your Dream Job* (Hoboken, NJ: John Wiley & Sons, 2009).

Noble, David. *Gallery of Best Cover Letters: Collection of Quality Cover Letters by Professional Resume Writers* (JIST Works, 2007).

Yate, Martin. *Knock 'em Dead Cover Letters* (Adams Media, 2008).

CHAPTER TWELVE

LOOKING FOR JOBS IN
ALL THE RIGHT PLACES

Every chapter of this book contains a list of resources that can help you connect with places to find jobs. Although each one of them is a good place to get started, they are not, by any means, the only way. This chapter explores other job search methods that may help you locate just the right position. Even if you lean toward one method more than another, don't rule any of them out. Each one has the potential to lead you to a job.

Searching the Ads

Display and classified advertisements are certainly one of the best places to get started. You can look locally, regionally, and nationally, depending on how far you want to go to track down your new career. Some potential places to look include:

- local city newspapers
- free community newspapers
- state publications
- trade publications
- professional publications
- bulletin boards at stores, colleges, and other institutions

If the job you are applying for is local, pursuing it is simple. Follow the directions in the ad. (Are you supposed to mail in a resume? Stop by the location in person? Call for an interview? Follow whatever the ad suggests.)

What if you are looking long distance, however? What if you want to move to a city or place but don't know what work is available? How do you do your job search in an area you do not currently live in? Here are some ideas:

- Find out as much about the place you'd like to move to as possible. The more you know about the place, the more you will know whether you really want to live there. You want to make sure that you can afford the cost of living there, as well as find out what the city is like in spirit and attitude. Study the climate—is it what you enjoy most? How much does housing cost in the area?

- Go online and see whether the city has an online version of its newspaper. Study the articles and check out the ads to see what kind of work is available. Who are the major employers in the area? Does the city specialize in one type of product or service? Watch the business section of the online paper to see what the trends are.

- If at all possible, make at least one trip to the area to scope it out and see if it matches what you had imagined and learned.

Going to Career/Job Fairs

Have you ever been to a job fair? When you were looking for a teaching job you might have attended one. Some of them are generic, while others are targeted to specific professions or industries. Regardless, they have the same purpose: A company gets the chance to meet and screen a large number of potential employees and you get the chance to find out a great deal about different companies and what they are looking for in workers. It's a win-win situation.

Randall Hansen, PhD at Quintessential Careers, offers the following tips for improving your chance of being selected at a job fair.

Preregister

More and more of these fairs offer this option, typically online. By registering in advance, you often have the opportunity to submit a resume. "Does preregistration guarantee that you will be noticed or that employers will even look at the registrations?" asks Hansen. "No, but why would you not take advantage of such an easy step?"

Research

Look at which companies will be at the fair so you can target the ones that most appeal to you.

Resumes

Bring a lot of them with you. If you have multiple kinds, each one designed for a different type of job, bring copies of each one. Better to have them and not need them than need them and not have them!

Portfolios

Bring these along, too. They should include your resume, a list of references, and samples of your best work.

Attire

First impressions cannot be undone. Don't show up in jeans and a T-shirt even if the job fair is for something casual like camp counselors. Be professional.

Strategy

Job fairs can be overwhelming, so go with a plan in hand. It is usually best to go and see your top choices first while you are still fresh and eager. However, if your top choices are shared by many others, you may face long lines. In that case, consider going to second choices until those lines slow down by the end of the day.

Interviewing

Typically you have between two and five minutes to make a great impression on a potential employer, so you have to work quickly and effectively. One of the most common questions you will be asked is, "What are you here for today?" so have a strong answer ready with which to respond. "A great concluding question for you to ask is, 'What do I need to obtain a second interview with your firm?'" writes Hansen.

Intangibles

Other quick tips include not taking time to interview with companies you have no real interest in working for, eavesdropping on others' interviews to pick up do's and don'ts to keep in mind when it is your turn, and reading company literature while you stand in line so you are informed by the time you get called.

Networking

Networking with recruiters is a given—that's why you are here. However, don't stop there. ". . . you can also network with your fellow job-seekers in terms of sharing information about job leads, companies and their recruiting strategies and styles," adds Hansen.

Follow-up

So few people do any follow-up that those who take the time tend to stand out. You can either call the recruiter the evening of the fair and leave a voice mail message thanking him for his time or you can send a more traditional thank-you note. "In the letter, thank the recruiter for his/her time, restate your interest and qualifications for the position, reiterate your interest in a second interview and make a promise to follow up the letter with a phone call (and then make sure you do in fact call)," adds Hansen.

Making Cold Calls

Cold calling is another job search method but it can be challenging. This style is an uninvited form of job hunting because you haven't been invited to get in touch with the person or organization beforehand.

Typically you begin the process by making the longest possible list of places you would like to approach for a job. Follow that up by gathering the names of the people in charge of hiring at each company. Sometimes you can get this information online (but often you won't know how up-to-date the site is). Experts advise that instead you call each company and ask the receptionist for the name of the hiring manager.

Next, you send one of those fantastic cover letters to each hiring manager (making sure each one is original, not a copy, of course). Finally, the next step is often the most intimidating—making the follow-up phone call. Call and refer to the letter you sent and then ask politely for an interview. You may likely be told that there are no current openings; if so, without being pushy, you can ask if you can still come in and interview in case things change in the future. The more interviews you can secure, the better your chances of finding a job.

"When you consider that four-fifths of the job market is 'closed,' meaning you can't find out about available job openings unless you dig for them—prospect for them, this method of job hunting takes on great importance."
—Randall Hansen, PhD, founder of Quintessential Careers

Volunteering Your Time

As you are searching for your new job, if you can afford it, consider doing some volunteering in your community. It can teach you new skills and supply you with new contacts, while you are also helping others and making a difference.

Volunteering has a number of advantages besides these. You have the chance to test a job environment without making a long-term commitment, and you are positioned to hear about job openings and can often be the first to apply for them.

Every community has a need for volunteers. To find what your area needs, check with local churches, schools, libraries, hospitals, camps, service organizations, and other institutions. They often publish lists on communal bulletin boards. Many city newspapers also feature regular columns listing organizations in search of volunteers.

In addition, many online sites list different volunteer needs throughout the country, so look through the resources section at the end of this chapter and do some exploring. For example, the National and Community Service site (http://www.nationalservice.gov/) has details about AmeriCorps, Senior Corps, Learn and Serve America, and more. Some sites combine pure volunteer needs with job opportunities as well, so be sure to look at those too (http://www.deepsweep.com/, http://www.execsearches.com, and http://www.opportunityknocks.org/ are three examples).

International sites post listings for volunteers to go to foreign countries. This gives you the chance to not only reap all the other benefits of volunteering, but also do some traveling. Check out the sites Global Volunteer Network

"Volunteering is fabulous strategy, especially for someone who does not have experience in the field they want to go into. You gain experience in a non-threatening way. It also gets you into a business industry where other people see you in action."

—Andrea Kay, author of *Life's a Bitch and Then You Change Careers: Nine Steps to Get Out of Your Funk and On to Your Future* (http://www.volunteer.org.nz/), Global Volunteers (http://www.globalvolunteers.org), and Habitat for Humanity International (http://www.habitat.org).

Going Online

As you can see from the information in this chapter, going online is one of the best ways to conduct a job search. In fact, research shows that more than four million job-related searches are conducted on Google every day. There is so much out there that you can spend hours each day exploring and learning about different opportunities. Of course, one of the most direct approaches is to look at job boards like Monster.com, Jobseekers.com, and so on. They are quite popular, although some experts predict that job boards may be on their way out.

What will replace job boards? According to Lou Adler, the man some refer to as the recruiting guru, the answer is something called talent hubs. These are smaller career sites that will list a class of jobs (marketing) rather than a specific job (senior product manager). Once someone shows interest, the candidates will be directed to more specific jobs or a chance to sign up with a company to find out about future opportunities. In addition, these new sites are going to offer other features such as forums, bulletin boards, games, polls, conference schedules, and more.

Another aspect of job searching that has undergone change is social networking venues such as MySpace, Facebook, LinkedIn, and Twitter. Experts predict that more and more potential job candidates will be recruited, assessed, and hired through these sites. Blogs have also become a source of potential job searching as they serve as a type of resume.

"A career change is a perfect time to build a skills set through volunteering, either enhancing what you already know or developing in a whole new direction."

—Laura Gassner Otting, author of *Change Your Career: Transitioning into the Nonprofit Sector*

The job search, regardless of which methods you use (and be sure to combine them—don't rely on just one!), is not typically a quick one. It takes time to figure out the details, make the right connections, and decide what you want to pursue. You went through the process at least once already when you chose a career in teaching—and now you are realizing it was not the ideal choice for you and it is time to do something different. This time around, do your homework and see if you can't choose something that is more on target with the adult you have become and the goals you want to accomplish.

"We have encountered no one in the last year who believes job boards are here to stay. Most experts predict they will be gone within 10 years, while some foresee their demise as soon as three years from now."

—Katherine Hansen, PhD

Further Resources to Investigate

Organizations

For volunteering

American Red Cross
http://www.redcross.org/

America's Charities
http://www.charities.org/

HandsOn Network
http://www.handsonnetwork.org/

Dress for Success
http://www.dressforsuccess.org/

4 Labors of Love
http://www.4laborsoflove.org/

Teach for America
http://www.teachforamerica.org/

For job searching

Career Builder
http://www.careerbuilder.com/?sc_cmp2=JS_Nav_Home

Career.com
http://www.career.com/

Hound
http://www.hound.com/

Indeed
http://hotjobs.yahoo.com/

Job Central
http://www.jobcentral.com/

Monster
http://home.monster.com/

Simply Hired
http://www.simplyhired.com/

Top School Jobs
http://www.topschooljobs.org/

Yahoo! Hot Jobs
http://www.indeed.com/Yahoo! Hot Jobs

For finding a career or job fair

Career Fairs
http://www.careerfairs.com/

Career Fairs Global
http://cfg-inc.com/

Job Expo
http://www.jobexpo.com/

Women for Hire
http://www.womenforhire.com/career_expos/

"A blog can establish you as an expert and thought-leader in your field, again raising your visibility with hiring decision-makers. Since blogs are updated regularly, you enhance your digital presence every time you blog."

—Katherine
   Hansen, PhD

Additional Reading

McClure, John. *Get the Job You Want: Practical Strategies for your Job Search Campaign* (Create Space, 2009).

Piotrowski, Katy. *Career Coward's Guide to Changing Careers: Sensible Strategies for Overcoming Job Search Fears* (JIST Works, 2007).

Sturm, Eric. *How to Manage a Successful Job Search: Tips from an Experienced Job Seeker* (Create Space, 2009).

CHAPTER THIRTEEN

NETWORKING:
IT'S ALL ABOUT WHO YOU KNOW

For years, the expression "It's not what you know but who you know" has been bandied about in the business world and elsewhere. When it comes to finding a job, this adage is especially true. Often the best job leads you get will come from someone you know, either professionally or personally. Some statistics state, in fact, that as many as 95 percent of job openings are hidden from the average job seeker and never advertised. The only way to find out about them is through word of mouth. With the years you have spent in the education world, you have most likely cultivated a decent number of contacts, both in your field and in others. This is the time to gather those resources and call in any favors. If you're a shy or introverted person, this can be a little challenging, but practice will help you improve and feel more comfortable.

Networking in Action

What exactly is networking? It is a somewhat nebulous term, but you are most likely networking when you go to any professional meeting, talk to others at public events, participate in community volunteer activities, stop by any social club or church, post online messages in forums and chat rooms, or simply talk to the person ahead of you in the grocery store line. In other words, networking happens whenever you communicate with someone, whether face to face, over the telephone, through an e-mail, or with a post on an Internet forum.

Who can be a potential contact for you? Make a list and see how many names you can put on it. Some people to consider:

"Friends, friends of friends, a barber, a neighbor and former co-workers are often the best resources for job seekers, especially in a market with far more people out of work than job openings."
—Kelly Pate, journalist

- family (think extended—aunts, uncles, cousins, godparents, etc.)
- friends (the close ones and the mere acquaintances)
- lawyer or accountant (any other people who provide professional services for you?)
- barber/stylist
- babysitter or child care provider
- current and former coworkers
- auto service technician
- children's teachers
- children's friends and parents
- current and former neighbors
- bowling league or other club members
- partner's employer and/or co-workers
- friends at church
- fellow volunteers at community charities
- college alumni
- personal or professional mentors
- customers/clients/vendors/suppliers

Once you have a list of names, think about how you want to phrase the fact that you are searching for a job. A straightforward approach is usually the best method. A simple, "Hey, I am on the lookout for a job in publishing. If you hear of anything, could you let me know?" is often enough. If you possibly can, emphasize that you are not asking for a job, but for information that will help you find a job. Ask for suggestions or ideas. Then, after you ask, be quiet and let the other person have the chance to respond.

In many cases, following up by providing a business card is a smart move. That way, if and when your contact does hear something, he or she has contact information at hand rather than having to search for it, or worse, hold onto the information until they see you again (which could be weeks to months). It gives the person a quick and easy way to contact you.

Just mentioning your job search once is not going to be enough, either. Without being redundant, bring it up regularly. If you talk to the person quite often, you will need to find unique ways of bringing it up ("I can't wait until I get that online teaching job" or "I have been studying for weeks so I can take that coaching job whenever it finally appears.")

It's also important that you take the time to reciprocate. Networking is about helping each other, so be willing to see the other person's need and fulfill it. Provide a resource, answer a question, give some advice—whatever you can to support the person you are talking to. It is just as important that you hone your listening skills as you develop your speaking skills. Be a good listener and discover how you can help other people and the networking process—in which you are most likely to be helped in return—will begin.

"When you network, it is imperative that you do not do all the talking. If you have asked another person for advice, make sure he or she has the opportunity to offer it. Also, when you do all the talking, the other person might feel confused and unsure of what action to take with the information you have supplied."

—Barbara Sahani, owner of Career Solvers

Networking Online

One of the most common methods of networking today, as mentioned in the previous chapter, is through social networks like Facebook, MySpace, Twitter, and LinkedIn. Do you think of those networks as something only for teens or young people hoping to find their soulmates? Think again. A report from ExecuNet stated that "60 percent of wealthy Americans with an average income of $287,000 per year and net worth of $2.1 million participate in online social networks, compared to just 27 percent a year ago."

". . . you must understand that you are networking every place you go. Networking is about building relationships. It's about learning things about other people. . . . People have had amazing experiences in their lives and it is great to hear about the wisdom they have gained and the challenges that they have overcome. What you want to do is ask questions and learn about the other person. You will be amazed at how quickly you will find a common ground between you. The key is when you ask a question, you have to listen to the answer. Then, you can build the answer to ask another question."
—Kathy Condon, "Career Communications" columnist

Here are some rules to follow when networking with others through these organizations:

- Connect only with the people who like you and will speak well of you.

- Be nice to your contacts—forwarding interesting articles, sharing job leads, and other gestures. Do unto others, right?

- Always remember that the Internet is worldwide. If you don't want certain information about you known, do not put in on the Web. One way or another, it will come back to haunt you. Do you really want a potential employer to see a photo of you at your best friend's bachelor party?

- Don't post information about the job or company online when you are still being considered for the position. Keep it to yourself.

- Always follow the rule of "netiquette;" that is, stay polite, watch your language, and be respectful of others.

A Two-Way Street

It is essential to keep in mind that networking is a sharing process. For it to work, it has to be beneficial to both people, otherwise you are just using other people for your own gain and that will establish a reputation that you certainly do not want. Leslie Smith from the National Association of Female Executives says that networking is the process of "planning and making contacts and sharing information for professional and personal gain." The key to successful networking is in the word sharing.

Networking is a term often used in the computer world to explain how the different systems are interconnected. One depends on the other in order to function properly. Perhaps this is also the case when networking occurs between people. In order to work their best, people must rely on the support of each other. What a great way to find a job—and live life!

Further Resources to Investigate

Organizations

Monster's Career Advice Forums
http://monster.prospero.com/monsterindex/

The Motley Fool's Ask the Headhunter
http://boards.fool.com/messages.asp?id=1040001000000000

Talk City
http://www.talkcity.com/

"The last place I want to pull applicants from is the classified ads of major newspapers. Classified ad applicants are unreferred, untested and unknown. The first place I look for applicants is within my current or previous organizations or applicants who were referred to me by professional colleagues and acquaintances. These applicants are better referenced, tested and known."

—J. O'Bruba, from
A Foot in the Door

Additional Reading

Baber, Anne, and Lynne Waymon. *Make Your Contacts Count: Networking Know-how for Business and Career Success* (AMACOM, 2007).

Levinson, Jay Conrad, and Monroe Mann. *Guerrilla Networking: A Proven Battle Plan to Attract the Very People You Want to Meet* (Author House, 2009).

Lowe, Doug. *Networking for Dummies* (John Wiley & Sons, 2009).

CHAPTER FOURTEEN

ENSURING INTERVIEWING SUCCESS

Just as there are a plethora of books and online materials out there on how to write successful cover letters and resumes, there are also quite a few resources on how to conduct a stellar interview. Check out what your libraries and bookstores have, as well as online sites. Let's take a look here anyway, and cover some of the most important points.

By the time you reach the interview, you have most likely already had limited contact with your potential employer. You've written a cover letter and compiled a resume and the employer has looked both of them over and deemed you worth further investigation. (Take a moment to celebrate—remember that statistic from earlier that only one interview is granted per 200 resumes submitted? That means while you are practicing for the interview, 199 people are feeling rather disappointed.)

Some companies will do online or telephone interviews—and these methods have their definite perks. You don't have to worry about whether your pantyhose have a run in them or whether you tied your tie properly, since no one can see you. However, you also don't have the chance to connect nearly as well as when you are face-to-face. So much for eye contact and your dazzling smile! Fortunately, most companies, even in this high-tech age, still rely on meeting you in person before making any official hiring decisions.

Let's break down the interview into three phases: before, during, and after. Each phase has its unique steps to follow and mistakes to avoid.

Before the Interview

- Learn all you can about the company or organization. It impresses bosses when you are already familiar with their services, and/or products. Go online and read through the different parts of their website (be sure to note any awards or accolades earned as they can be great to throw in as you chat). If you have any pamphlets or brochures from a career fair, look through those as well.

- Be ready to answer difficult questions. Even if you don't have the answer prepared, if you keep your cool and stay calm no matter what someone asks, you will earn points.

- Have your paperwork handy in case they want to see it again. Some examples to bring along are your Social Security card, a copy of your resume, your driver's license, the completed job application, any personal or professional references, and, if applicable, your transcripts.

- Practice answering typical interview questions (see box) with a friend or someone you trust so that your answers sound confident and smooth.

- Make sure you have a professional outfit to wear and that it is clean, pressed and ready to go.

- Leave cigarettes and chewing gum at home so you won't be tempted to use either one.

- Map out where the business is so you can drive there without confusion or being late because you got lost.

- Make sure you know how to pronounce the name of the person who is interviewing you, if you've been given the information.

- Avoid using strong perfumes/colognes, wearing loud jewelry, or having any other tangible distractions in your attire.

- Make a list of several questions you want to ask the interviewer. They want to see that you have given the job thought and want to know more about it.

- Get a good night's sleep the night before and eat a meal before going to the interview (but don't drip anything on your shirt, and check your teeth in the bathroom before the interview starts).

During the Interview

- Give a firm handshake to the person who is interviewing you.

- Make direct eye contact.

- Avoid slang and never curse.

- Answer any and all questions honestly and clearly. Never lie.

- Be enthusiastic about the business and the position.

- Sit up straight.

- Ask for clarification if you do not understand a question.

- When done, thank the interviewer and shake hands once again.

- Request a business card from the interviewer before leaving.

- Keep your cell phone turned off for the entirety of the interview.

"You can always leave this bit of modern life in your car, but if you must take it with you, make sure it stays turned off and in your briefcase; it's a huge sign of disrespect to be interrupted during an interview or give the appearance you'll be interrupted."

—Christine Della Monaca, Monster staff writer

After the Interview

- Send a thank-you card.
- Do any other follow-up that was mentioned in the interview (call back after so many days, create a writing sample, etc.).

Typical Interview Questions

- Why do you want to work here?
- What are your greatest strengths?
- What are your biggest weaknesses?
- Why did you leave your last job?
- What do you see yourself doing five years from now?
- Why did you choose this career/to change careers?
- Why should I hire you?
- What can you tell us about our company?
- Tell me a little about yourself.
- Do you have any questions for me?
- What salary are you hoping for?
- What can you do for us that someone else can't do?
- What new skills have you developed recently?
- What is important to you in a job?
- What qualities do you find important in your coworkers?
- What have you learned from your past jobs?
- Whom may we contact for references?

Your interview is the chance for you to get a feel for the employer and the business and the employer to get a feel about your abilities and job qualifications. Not every interview will result in a job offer and if it doesn't, don't spend time berating yourself and wondering what you could have done differently. Competition is often fierce and not getting a job offer isn't a reflection of you (although it can be if you made some huge mistakes), so learn from whatever you can and then change your shoes and get ready for the next interview.

Further Resources to Investigate

Additional Reading

Allen, Jeffrey. *Instant Interviews: 101 Ways to Get the Best Job of Your Life* (John Wiley & Sons, 2009).

Beshara, Tony. *Acing the Interview: How to Ask and Answer the Questions that will Get You the Job* (AMACOM, 2008).

Burns, Daniel. *The First 60 Seconds: Win the Job Interview before it Begins* (Sourcebooks, 2009).

Dorio, Mark. *The Complete Idiot's Guide to the Perfect Job Interview, 3rd edition* (Alpha Books, 2009).

CHAPTER FIFTEEN

SAYING GOOD-BYE

The day has finally arrived for you. You've spent weeks, even months, contemplating the idea of leaving teaching. After all, it is not an easy decision and should not be taken lightly.

You've explored different career options, done your homework on what other jobs require, researched professional possibilities, and winnowed the list down to the two or three options that appeal to you most.

You've already started the job search, looking online at different company websites, contacting others in the field, and scanning through national and local job boards, and you're ready to move forward. But you have one more step to take care of before you can do that. You have to let your school know that you are resigning and switching career paths. Could you just walk in and say, "I quit! Bye"? It depends on your contract and what it spells out as far as quitting. But even if there is nothing in it to stop you from doing this, it's a rotten idea. Not only is it rude, as it leaves your school scrambling to cover for you, but it is unkind to your students as well. It shows a lack of respect for all involved. Moreover, it is creating a bad reputation for you that you simply do not want. If you had planned to get a referral from your principal, this kind of attitude would most likely cancel that. Don't burn your bridges behind you because you never know when you are going to have to double back and cross them again.

Let's explore the ways to make leaving your school as painless for everyone as possible.

Legally, What Are Your Obligations?

The first step in quitting is pulling out your contract and reading through it carefully to see what terms and conditions are in place. Although contracts do tend to be similar, yours may include some elements that are not mentioned here. Experts recommend that before you actually walk in and make your official resignation announcement you should consult your lawyer and have her look over your contract to ensure you have not missed anything important. Things to look for in your contract include:

- If you were only recently hired at the school, does your contract include anything about a probationary period? (They typically last one to three months.) If so, are you leaving before the period is over? If so, this can be dicey, so talk to your lawyer about your legal options.

- The section of the contract that is often labeled "Notice" is your most important portion to read through. It will typically spell out the amount of notice you have to give your employer before leaving (usually two weeks to a month). In some cases, that time period may change depending on the time of year. Quitting in June makes it far easier for the administration to find a replacement than if you quit in October. Other facts to note: Will you continue to be paid during your notice period and will it be different from your usual salary? Can your employer ask you to leave before the end of your notice period? If he does—and you do—will you still be paid for that time period?

- What other benefits did this job offer (i.e. health insurance coverage, unused vacation and sick pay, stock options, 401k and pension plans)? Will you be able to take any of them with you?

"Tell your students and co-workers that you are quitting. Even though it is not formally required, give all parties with whom you have a personal or close professional relationship verbal notice that you will be leaving."
—R.A. Anderson, eHow contributing writer

Once you know what stipulations your contract has, be sure to follow them. As long as you follow the terms of your contract, your employer has no choice but to accept your resignation. Be sure to return any company property that you might have including keys to classrooms, parking passes, computers, and so on. Remove all of your personal items and files from the workplace.

Creating a Resignation Letter

Most people in the educational and related fields tend to resign through an official letter. What do you say? What don't you say? Let's look at a basic format to follow and list some do's and don'ts.

- DO make it professional and error free.
- DO show appreciation for the time spent at the school.
- DO ask for a letter of reference to take with you before you leave.
- DO emphasize how the job has benefited you and what you have learned.
- DO include the last day you will be in the classroom.
- DO make a copy for the principal, as well as payroll and human resources. Keep one for yourself as well.
- DO NOT say anything negative about your coworkers, the school, or the administration.
- DO NOT use this letter to air any grievances you had while working at the school.
- DO NOT include the specifics of where you are going next as it may change.

Here is a basic resignation letter template. Following the list above, feel free to customize it as fits your situation.

Your Name
Your Address
Your E-mail

Date

Principal's Name
School Name
Address

Dear _____,
It has been a pleasure to work at _____ School for (months/years). I have learned a great deal from the experience. I appreciate the guidance, support, and encouragement I have been given by fellow teachers and the administration during my time here.

However, I have decided that it is time for me to move on in another direction. This letter is my formal resignation from my teaching position at _____ School. In fulfillment of my contract, I am giving you _____ (weeks/month) notice from today's date of _____. My last working day will be _____.

I wish you and everyone at _____ School continued success.

Sincerely,

Your Signature
cc: Human Resources, Payroll

Hand deliver the letter so that it does not get lost in someone's inbox during the hectic daily mail shuffle.

How the principal and other people within the administration respond to your resignation depends entirely on their personalities, your relationship, and many other factors. You may be offered a good-bye party—or not. You may have people miserable that you are leaving—or doing high fives behind your back (hopefully not!). The principal may accept your resignation without a fight—or immediately give you a counter offer with better terms and conditions. How you respond to any of this is up to you, but the best advice is the same regardless: stay respectful, listen patiently to any final words.

When you finally do pack up all your things, say good-bye to everyone who is important to you, and head out to the parking lot for the last time, take a deep breath and look ahead to the future. A new career and all its infinite possibilities are ahead of you. Who knows what adventures are right around the corner?

"Life is either a great adventure or nothing."
—Helen Keller

Further Resources to Investigate

Additional Reading

Eisaguirre, Lynne. *Tough Conversations with your Boss: From Promotions to Resignations* (Adams Media, 2009).

Sack, Steven Mitchell. *Getting Fired: What to Do if You're Fired, Downsized, Laid Off, Restructured, Discharged, Terminated or Forced to Resign* (Grand Central Publishing, 2000).

BIBLIOGRAPHY

Adams, Margaret. *How to Take Charge of Your Teaching Career* (New York: Continuum International Publishing Group, New York, 2008).

Anderson, R.A. "How to Quit a Teaching Job". Ehow.com. http://www.ehow.com/how_5171261_quit-teaching-job.html

Author unknown. "How to Avoid Overseas Job Scams." Overseas Digest. http://www.overseasdigest.com/scams.htm

Author unknown. "All-Stars: The Greatest Hits from Six Years of Resumes." Mekong Network. http://www.mekong.net/tech/resmhits.htm

Blackwell, Kelly. "Teaching Overseas: Are You the Right Person for the Job?" Overseas Digest. http://www.overseasdigest.com/teaching-abroad/right-person-for-teaching-abroad.htm

Bryan, E. Chandlee. "Five Strategies for Leveraging Your Online Social Networks." Quintessential Careers.com. www.quintcareers/printable/leveraging_social_networks_html

Chaika, Glori. "International Teaching: What is it Really Like?" Education World. com/ Overseas Digest. http://www.overseasdigest.com/teaching-overseas-really-like.htm

Condon, Kathy. "Career Networking Explained: Making Connections, Building Relationships." Quintessential Careers.com. www.quintcareers.com/printable/career_networking_explained.html

Crary, David. "Stuttering Kids Taste Stardom at Arts Camp," August 25, 2009, MSN News. http://www.msnbc.msn.com/id/32553108/ns/health/

Della Monaca, Christine. "Interview Take Along Checklist." Monster.com. http://career-advice.monster.com/job-interview/interview-preparation/interview-take-along-checklist/article.aspx

Edelfelt, Roy, EdD, and Alan Reiman EdD. *Careers in Education* (New York: McGraw-Hill, 2004).

Edwards, Jim. "Web Casting: The Future of Online Education." Teachnology.com. www.teach-nology.com/tutorials/webcast/

Feirson, Robert and Seth Weitzman. *How to Get the Teaching Job You Want* (Stylus Publishing: Virginia) 2004.

Gisler, Margaret. *101 Career Alternatives for Teachers* (California: Prima Publishing, 2002).

Hansen, Katharine, Ph.D. "Cover Letter FAQs and the Competitive Edge in the Job Market." Quintessential Careers.com. http://www.quintcareers.com/printable/edge.html#ten

Hansen, Katherine, PhD. "Frequently Asked Questions (FAQs) about Career Networking." Quintessential Career.com. www.quintcareers.com/printable/career_networking_FAQ.html

Hansen, Katharine, PhD. "How to Get Started on Your Resume: A Five Step Primer for Established Job Seekers and Career Changers." Quintessential Careers.com. http://www.quintcareers.com/printable/job-seeker_resume_primer.html

Hansen, Katharine, PhD. "The Long, Slow Death March of Job Boards—and What Will Replace Them." Quintessential Careers.com. http://www.quintcareers.com/job-board_death_march.html

Hansen, Randall, PhD. "The Ten Keys to Success at Job and Career Fairs." Quintessential Careers.com. www.quintcareers.com/printable/job_career_fairs.html

Hobgood, Bobby. "Becoming an Online Teacher." Learn NC.com. http://www.learnnc.org/lp/pages/665

Jones, Elka. "You're a What? Image Consultant." *Occupational Outlook Quarterly*. Fall 2005. http://www.bls.gov/opub/ooq/2005/fall/yawhat.pdf

LearningExpress. *Becoming a Teacher* (New York: LearningExpress, 2009).

Pate, Kelly. "Everyday People Key in Job Networking." Denver Post (March 30, 2003) www.rileyguide.com/network.html

Sahana, Barbara M.A., CERW, NCRW, CPRW, CCM. "Seven Rules for Networking Success." Quintessential Careers.com. www.quintcareers.com/printable/networking_success.html

Starkey, Lauren M.A., *Change your Career: Teaching as Your New Profession* (New York: Kaplan Publishing, 2007).

Thompson, Mary Anne. *The Global Resume and CV Guide* (Hoboken: Wiley, 2000).

Thompson, Mary Anne. "How to Create a 'Culturally Correct' CV." Overseas Digest.com. http://www.overseasdigest.com/globalcv.htm

Valle, Joan Della, and Emmet Sawyer. *Teacher Career Starter* (New York: LearningExpress, 2002).

White, Ross. "Four Myths about Online Learning." Learn NC.com. http://www.learnnc.org/lp/pages/2720

ABOUT THE AUTHOR

Tamra Orr is a full-time writer and author living in the Pacific Northwest. She has written more than 200 nonfiction books for readers of all ages. She graduated from Ball State University in Muncie, Indiana and began her career as a high school English teacher. After she married and had her first of four children, she merged into the publishing world as a freelancer and has never looked back. Today she uses her teaching experience to write books and quiz her kids daily.

NOTES

NOTES

NOTES

NOTES

NOTES

NOTES

NOTES